A WATERED GARDEN

The LORD shall guide thee continually, and satisfy thy soul in drought, . . . thou shalt be like a watered garden, and like a spring of water, whose waters fail not (Isa. 58:11 KJV).

ALICE HUFF and **ELEANOR BURR** serve on the Homeland Staff of OMS International, a nondenominational mission agency with headquarters in Indianapolis. Alice Huff is executive director of World Intercessors, which sponsors prayer retreats and coordinates a prayer support network for missionaries. Eleanor Burr edits the OMS OUTREACH, a monthly magazine, and was formerly president of the Evangelical Press Association.

A WATERED GARDEN

Devotional Stories from Missionaries

Compiled by
Alice Huff and Eleanor Burr

Special Edition
OMS International, Inc.
P.O. Box A
Greenwood, Indiana 46142

FRANCIS ASBURY PRESS is an imprint of
Zondervan Publishing House
1415 Lake Drive, S.E.
Grand Rapids, Michigan 49506

Library of Congress Cataloging in Publication Data

A Watered garden.
    1. Missionary stories. 2. Devotional calendars. I. Huff, Alice. II. Burr, Eleanor.
BV2087.W34 1987   242'.2   87-1056
ISBN 0-310-39390-6

All Scripture quotations, unless otherwise noted, are taken from the *Holy Bible: New International Version* (North American Edition), copyright © 1973, 1978, 1984, by the International Bible Society. Used by permission of Zondervan Bible Publishers.

Scripture quotations marked AMP. are taken from *The Amplified Bible,* copyright © 1965 by Zondervan Publishing House. Used by permission of Zondervan Bible Publishers.

Scripture quotations marked LB are taken from *The Living Bible,* copyright © 1971 by Tyndale House Publishers, Wheaton, Illinois.

Scripture quotations marked PHILLIPS are taken from *The New Testament in Modern English*, revised edition, copyright © 1958, 1960, 1972 by J. B. Phillips and published by The Macmillan Company.

Designed by Louise Bauer
Edited by Thelma Lawrence and Joseph D. Allison

Printed in the United States of America

Fourth Printing, 1994

HOW "A WATERED GARDEN" CAME TO BE

With Japanese evangelist Juji Nakada, Charles and Lettie Cowman opened a Bible training institute in Tokyo in April 1901. Nakada wanted his large number of converts educated for ministry. In 1902, Ernest and Julia Kilbourne joined the team. They recognized that only through indigenous workers could Japan ever be reached for Christ.

Nightly evangelistic meetings resulted in fifteen thousand Japanese converts in ten years. Training classes soon captured the zeal of these new believers. Eager to proclaim their newfound faith, they quickly acquired skills to draw other Japanese people to their Savior. The Cowmans issued a plea to the small band of supporting friends back home: "Send young men from Bible schools across North America to help us." Ten workers responded.

Through what they labeled "The Great Village Campaign," they teamed these workers with several Japanese trainees from their second-floor Bible school in Tokyo. With carefully sectioned maps, they dispersed them across the islands. The workers' assignment: Reach every creature with a Gospel portion, a personal witness of Christ's claims, and an opportunity to respond through nightly evangelistic tent meetings.

Within seven years, these teams completely covered Japan. They reached 10,300,000 homes and established hundreds of thriving Christian congregations. God led the Kilbourne-Cowman team to repeat this then-unique method of missionary outreach in Korea (1907) and in China (1925). Their work was incorporated in 1910 as The Oriental Missionary Society.

World War II closed those doors, leaving a number of OMS missionaries in concentration camps. Those who safely returned to their homelands, however, soon saw God's finger pointing to Latin America. A broad constituency evolved to support their efforts in Colombia, Ecuador, and Brazil.*

In 1918 Mr. Cowman suffered a massive heart attack, ending his tireless push to reach those "who still haven't heard." Through long nights of agony in which he could neither recline nor sleep, his gaze seldom left the huge map muraled across his Los Angeles bedroom wall. In prayer he paved roadways from city to city, begging God for more workers to penetrate the uttermost parts of the world with God's Word.

Eager to comfort her dying husband, Mrs. Cowman searched libraries and bookstores for words of solace. As the writings of fellow Christians and earlier saints lifted their spirits, Mrs. Cowman realized the purpose of her husband's confinement. Gathering the tidbits and clippings that had ministered to them, she compiled what have become the best selling devotional books of all time: *Streams in the Desert, Springs in the Valley,* and *Consolation.*

Could it be that OMS missionaries who follow in the

*Now known as OMS International, the Cowmans' organization includes 431 missionaries from six nations, 4,052 trained national workers, and 2,738 established congregations in fourteen countries. Homeland offices in Canada, Australia, New Zealand, the British Isles, South Africa, and the United States keep the overseas workers linked with those who pledge financial and prayer backing. The same distinctives—evangelism, training native workers, and establishing self-supporting churches—still characterize OMS.

Cowmans' footsteps are to carry on this ministry of healing, encouragement, and hope through their devotional writings? Current reader response indicated it was true. This spurred us to rendezvous at a Florida condo owned by mutual friends. There, while Eleanor's husband recuperated from triple bypass surgery, we pored over accumulated manuscripts, daily claiming divine guidance in our selections of meditations and related Scriptures.

Our task gained momentum as we pondered our unique privilege. Neither of us recalled a devotional book designed to express the excitement and obligation of God's global command. Who better to challenge the drifting believer than those who have responded to Jesus' mandate, "Go ye into all the world"?

These missionaries' discoveries propel the reader to new understanding and involvement as a world Christian. In addition, their unveiling of their own frailties and failures shows missionaries to be fallible humans, longing for supportive prayer. In a new way, the reader can sense the obligation—indeed, the urgency—to fortify overseas workers with intercession and personal support.

These missionaries have proved God's promises through the normal vicissitudes of life, while enduring the frustrations and privations of living in foreign cultures. The writings flow from their experiences while "toughing it out" in the dark places of earth.

The title, *A Watered Garden,* springs from Isaiah 58:11 (see frontispiece). It also seems a natural sequel to Mrs. Cowman's *Streams* and *Springs.* As the Christian discovers God's streams along his pilgrimage and springs of joy to carry him through the valley days, he matures into fruit-bearing fulfillment "like a watered garden, whose waters fail not."

Alice Huff and Eleanor Burr
OMS International

WEEK 1/SUNDAY

WE DON'T HAVE TO RETURN

Your attitude should be the same as that of Christ Jesus ... taking the very nature of a servant ... he humbled himself and became obedient to death (Phil. 2:5–8).

Across South Korea, Colonel Lee is known as the foremost fighter pilot. I was somewhat awed to be in his presence. But the illness of his daughter put us on common ground and, as her nurse, I became well-acquainted with his family.

Although Colonel Lee was not a Christian, we often talked about spiritual matters and prayed. I enlisted the prayers of others on his behalf. Sometime after his daughter's discharge from the hospital, Colonel Lee phoned me and said, "I had to let you know that this morning I took Jesus Christ into my heart. Now I belong to Him." My heart throbbed with excitement. Great evangelistic potential is wrapped up in this man.

I have often been challenged by one of our conversations. We had talked about his assignment in case of attack from North Korea. At a moment's notice, it would be his duty to fly his plane the farthest north. I asked, "Colonel, do you think you would return from that kind of mission?"

"Not a chance," he said. "With their missiles, it would be impossible. But we have our assignment to go."

"How do you feel about that?" I continued.

"If and when I'm needed, I'm ready to go."

While on a recent furlough, my husband, J.B., presented our slides of Korea to a church group. Among the slides was a picture of the "Bridge of No Return" at Panmunjom. Beyond that bridge stretches a desolate valley

9

of "no man's land" where only guards can cross from South to North Korea. J.B. told the congregation, "No one from South Korea is permitted to cross that bridge, but I'm praying that soon we will cross it with the gospel." His statement jolted me. From what I knew about North Korea, this seemed dangerous and impossible.

Soon afterward, I read an article by the first Western reporter who has been permitted to enter North Korea in the past twenty-one years. He said that he had never seen such hatred in the eyes of five- and six-year-olds. In his opinion, it would take another generation or two before Americans could have any relationship with the North Koreans. Since J.B. was away in another meeting, I mailed him a copy of the article.

Soon we were in another church meeting, and he repeated his statement about planning to go to North Korea. I quizzed him afterward. Had he not read the article? He had, and he felt that the reporter's observations were likely true. But he had confidence that God could lead American missionaries across that bridge.

At that moment, Colonel Lee's words came to my mind: "If and when I'm needed, I'm ready to go." He would not hesitate, even though it would mean his life.

God dealt with me. He asked whether I was willing to cross the Bridge of No Return, even if it meant no return for me. I fell on my knees that night and stayed in prayer until I could match Colonel Lee's dedication.

Christ commanded us to go. He didn't say we had to return.

—Bette Crouse/South Korea

WEEK 1/MONDAY

NO TEARS TOMORROW

The LORD has been good. . . . For you, O LORD, have delivered my soul from death, my eyes from tears, my feet from stumbling (Ps. 116:7–8).

Stooping by the brook of Kerith, Elijah came face-to-face with starvation (1 Kings 17). No dew or rain was to be in sight for several years, and it was frightening to scoop up the last drops of water. Was God's providence really working for him?

When do we say, "How providential"? Is it when someone we love has been spared, a prayer answered, a wish granted, an undertaking completed, a desperate need met? Is *providence* simply another word for getting what we ask or being able to complete our plans?

It's easier to recognize the love that gives than the love that takes. But in the education of faith, we learn of a providence of loss, a ministry of fading and failing things, a gift of emptiness. A desperate situation can change into a notable blessing when we reach the end of our resources and meet God at the beginning of His.

Elijah's account pictures the progress of God's providence, from abundance to want. Divinely led to Kerith, he was fed there for a time. But then the brook dried up. If he could have seen the widow's cottage at Zarephath, with the oil and the meal that would not fail, he would have felt no test. But God builds the final success of His people on the basis of temporary failure. We do not learn some things until we walk in the borderland of need, until we live for awhile beside a failing brook in a famished land.

Had Elijah walked straight to Zarephath, we would be without the Bible's description of his prayer of faith: "Elijah

11

was a man just like us. He prayed earnestly that it would not rain, and it did not rain on the land for three and a half years. Again he prayed, and the heavens gave rain, and the earth produced its crops" (James 5:17–18).

What light does Elijah's story cast on our experiences? Many of us have been, or are at, the waterless brook of Kerith. A loss of employment, an unexpected sorrow, a persistent sense of loneliness, frustrations in our personal relationships—any of these create turmoil and hurt. Our outlook brightens, however, when we understand that God leads us *through* hard places; He doesn't keep us there. They are merely stages of our journey, and tomorrow will explain today.

All of us can say, "The Lord gave." Some of us must add, "And the Lord has taken away." If we are faithful and patient, however, someday we'll find that He has given double for all of our losses.

Whatever your stance in life, have faith in God. Pray without ceasing. And give thanks for everything. Whether His providence is obscure or clear, it is always at work in your life—full of love, and right in the end. Remember that the tears of life belong to the interlude, not the finale, of your story.

—Alice Huff/United States

WEEK 1/TUESDAY

WHEN I COULDN'T TAKE IT

Against all hope, [he] in hope believed (Rom. 4:18).

"Joanna, you have a ruptured disc in your back," the doctor said as I winced in my Tokyo hospital bed. "We'll give it six weeks in traction. If that doesn't help, you'll have to consider returning to the States."

I knew I was in trouble; my big toes were already numb and the leg pain was severe. Similar suffering had sent me back to the United States for surgery before. Agonizing memories of that long flight, and of being shifted on a stretcher to an Indianapolis hospital, had not been erased from my mind.

During this term of service in Japan, I had had faith that I would suffer no major illness. We still had several months to go, yet here I was. Suspended in traction, I received injections every three hours, but nothing killed the pain. And X-rays revealed extensive damage.

One morning I cried to the Lord, "I can't take it any longer. Father, I give it all to You!"

Immediately, the pain left. I could hardly contain myself for joy. I told the nurses, but they did not believe me. My doctor responded, "This is serious business. Let us not push God."

For two more days, I remained in bed, but without medication for pain. When another doctor visited me, I convinced him to let me try to walk. He took me to the therapy room for an examination. Large tears filled his eyes as he said, "This is the first miracle I have seen . . . other than when a soul has come to Christ." He summoned the head surgeon, who was also surprised by his findings. As the news traveled through the hospital, nurses scurried in to see me. That afternoon I walked out of the hospital.

Our seventeen-year-old Becky said, "Mother, I can't believe it. I prayed and prayed for you, but I guess I didn't really believe God would do it."

God brought His help in a way that enabled everyone to see His power. He knew my strength, measured it to the last inch, and did not allow me more than I could bear. He also took all the faith I possessed. The amount of my faith was not the key; but the fact that I placed all my faith in Him was.

—Joanna Dyer/Japan

WEEK 1/WEDNESDAY

HE'S ALWAYS WITH ME

Look carefully then how you walk! Live purposefully and worthily and accurately, not as the unwise and witless, but as wise—sensible, intelligent people; making the very most of the time—buying up each opportunity—because the days are evil (Eph. 5:15–16 AMP.).

The mountains offered us a much-needed break from language study. But as we left those cool, quiet heights and drove into the hot and teeming city, I felt my peace ebbing away. Dodging the countless cars and motorcycles, I realized that a scowl now creased my forehead.

"Oh, Lord," I whispered, "please take away my tension."

Home at last, Glen and I unloaded the car. Knowing that we would have guests shortly, I had asked our children to keep the living room in order. I was filled with disbelief. The shedding cat slept comfortably on my newly washed couch cushions. The brown rug bristled with cat hair. Our fourteen-year-old Greg's jigsaw puzzle lay scattered about. The jangling telephone insisted that we pick up our daughter from a birthday party.

As I ran our bags upstairs, I prayed again, "Lord, be my strength and peace right now. Please take control."

With lightning speed, I ran the sweeper and disposed of cat, kids, and puzzle. That left thirty minutes to shower and change before Peter arrived with his teacher. (Peter is a young Chinese soldier that Glen led to the Lord last summer.) Just as I undressed for the shower, the doorbell rang and I heard Greg say, "Hi, Peter!"

"Oh, no!" I moaned. "Not yet!" Glen and I looked at each other in despair. "Be down in a minute!" I called.

Quickly washing my face and changing my clothes, I dashed downstairs. There sat, not only Peter and his teacher, but his teacher's new wife. This meant I would need to entertain her while the men discussed their business. When would I prepare the snacks for our Taiwanese youth group, due to arrive in two hours?

"Nevertheless, not my will but Yours, Lord," I prayed— just as Glen suggested that I show Mrs. Tsai around the house.

She spoke no English, so I forced my frazzled brain to try to communicate in Chinese. She was so sweet that soon I was actually enjoying our little tour. We entered the living room to find Glen and Mr. Tsai in earnest conversation. As they turned to greet us, joy glowed in their faces.

"Sit down," Glen said. "Mr. Tsai wants to pray and receive Christ."

Later Mr. Tsai said, "I have many troubles, but I know Jesus will always be with me." I heard the same words echo in my own heart.

—Diana Francis/Taiwan

WEEK 1/THURSDAY

INTERCEDING IN THE GARDEN

*Your attitude must be like my own, for I, the Messiah,
did not come to be served, but to serve (Matt. 20:28 LB).*

Confusion and frustration flooded my tiny bedroom. A
multitude of perplexities bombarded me. I faced one of
those situations that made me want to run. But where
could I go?

As I prayed about my situation, God brought vividly into
focus the face of Eleanor Burr, who had been a great
source of blessing to me during my Asbury College years.
"Pray for her instead of yourself," the Holy Spirit challenged
me. As I began praying for Eleanor, I discovered a new joy.
My own anguish began to disappear as I visualized victory
in Eleanor's life, resulting from my prayers.

I continued this practice for several months until the
Holy Spirit led me to write to Eleanor. I obeyed the leading,
though I did not know her very well. I felt sure that she was
unaware of how God had influenced me through her life.
But Eleanor's response brought tears to my eyes. "Now I
know why these past months have been the best in my
life," she wrote. "Overwhelming problems have seemingly
faded away."

Job wrote of having his captivity turned to freedom
when he prayed for his friends. Mine was a similar
experience.

The reward of praying for others is unparalleled. I had
locked myself in the dungeon of self-pity; but God called
me into the throne room of intercession. This timely
preparation helped me to face my father's sudden death a
month later and, within a year, to surmount my brother's
severe illness. Ever since, major and minor crises have
subsided as I prayed for others.

This truth is not new. Jesus prayed for you and me—for all those who would come to believe in Him—during His hour of greatest crisis (John 17:20). Is there any greater example of interceding for others at a time of critical personal need? Are we not bidden to follow His example?

If you want to experience Calvary love, enter your Garden of Gethsemane and allow the Holy Spirit to intercede through you for someone else. After that, you will not want to confront perplexity in any other way.

—Jeannine Brabon/Spain

WEEK 1/FRIDAY

ON THE OTHER SHORE

Pray for each other so that you may be healed (James 5:16).

My eyes couldn't hold the torrent surging from my heart. The overflow dropped across the incredible words on the floral notepaper in my hand.

"I thought I should let you know that this past year you have been my prayer target," the letter said. "With every problem I've faced—physical, emotional, spiritual, material—instead of praying for myself I've been impressed to pray for you in that same area of need."

Of course! That's why this year topped all that I had known! I had not been able to understand it before; but now the events of the year took the shape of a breathtaking tapestry.

The painful rift in a cherished relationship had somehow healed. Love and helpfulness now replaced the stinging words.

On my job, material had arrived in time to meet impossible deadlines. And when the workload seemed unbearable, someone with exactly the right skills always "happened" to come by and help me.

Our adopted Korean daughter, plagued with rejection and taunts by her peers, had suddenly gained their acceptance and respect.

For years, I had fretted about my inability to witness. And what a flood of victories God had sent that year—the salvation of a terminally ill neighbor, God's answer for a divorcee whom I'd met on a cross-country flight, countless bedside conversations in a nursing home.

On and on the list went—spectacular answers, not to

my prayers, but to those selflessly flowing from a young missionary woman then serving in Colombia. "This has been the toughest year of my life," the letter continued. "But as I focused prayer on you, God miraculously resolved my problems as well."

Never can I adequately express my gratitude to Jeannine Brabon for that note and for the prayer secret it revealed. Over and over again, I've discovered the truth of this principle from God's Word. It's the same in prayer as in all other aspects of daily life: "Help another's boat across the waves and, lo, thine own has reached the other shore."

—Eleanor L. Burr/United States

WEEK 1/SATURDAY

A SECOND OPINION

I have heard your prayer . . . I will heal you (2 Kings 20:5).

"I think my arm's broken!" Mark rushed through the door, tears streaming, his left arm hanging limp and misshapen.

Mark stood there, obviously in pain, yet he seemed more anxious about my reaction. How many times I had warned him about his reckless adventures—climbing trees, jumping fences, and carelessly riding bicycles! "I just fell!" he wailed.

I had set many broken arms and legs at our clinic, so I quickly examined Mark's arm and made a temporary splint to brace it. It was almost dark when we arrived at the clinic. X-rays showed a bad break and dislocation. So I struggled to forget that I was Mark's father and tried to become just the doctor with another broken bone to set. "Help me, Lord," I prayed.

With the help of nurse Flo Boyer, I laid Mark back on the small X-ray table and gave him an anesthetic. The heat of the tropic night and my inner tension sent perspiration rolling off my body. After a long, difficult manipulation, I raised up and said, "Surely the bones are in position now."

But another X-ray showed the elbow was still far from right. The whole process had to be repeated. Another anesthetic was given, and I exerted an even stronger pull and push on the arm. More confident, I applied a cast to the arm as we waited for another X-ray.

I had to face the truth then. The arm was worse than I thought. The X-ray showed that the brachial artery might be ruptured. I knew the results of similar breaks: sometimes a useless arm, sometimes amputation. We had to get Mark to a large hospital with better facilities.

The next morning, Mark and I flew to Miami. His arm had swollen to twice its normal size; his hand had turned blue and cold. The admitting physician looked at the arm and said little. He could detect no pulse in it. He needn't tell me anything; I knew.

With a heavy heart, I phoned our mission headquarters and asked them to alert our prayer families about Mark's need. Many times I had prayed for our patients in Haiti, and the Lord had often healed. Now my faith knew greater testing.

On the fourth morning, I walked into Mark's room and instinctively felt for his pulse. There it was—ever so faint, a tiny throb. Once again, life-giving blood circulated through the arm. The Lord had started the healing process.

I will ever remember the trusting prayers of God's people, who know the Great Physician. We can use all of our medical skills, all of the knowledge God has given us; but only the Lord heals. And He heals in answer to prayer.

—Dr. Stafford Bourke/Haiti

WEEK 2/SUNDAY

ON SHORT NOTICE

Seek first his kingdom and his righteousness, and all these things will be given to you as well (Matt. 6:33).

Vivian was her name. With a friendly smile but a touch of formality, she greeted us at the door. Three children had been spying from the window as we approached, and now she introduced us. Wally, Kenny, Nanette—ages thirteen, ten, and nine—had obviously just come back from adventures in rain puddles. Grinning from ear to ear, they welcomed us like friendly puppies. Their daddy, they announced, was at work until after midnight.

Vivian filled two cups from a steaming pot of coffee and pulled out chairs at the kitchen table. Her mobile home did not have room for the neighborhood meeting she had scheduled that night, so she had arranged it at a neighbor's house. Because she had no room for overnight accommodations, we would be staying with a nearby elderly lady. As she outlined these plans, Vivian's voice carried no hint of apology or embarrassment.

The next morning, Vivian met us in her well-used station wagon. She drove us to visit a shut-in, then back to her own trailer home, where husband Walter greeted us warmly. The coffee cups were filled again and we began getting acquainted with Walter, who had accepted Christ just four days earlier.

Suddenly, a car pulled into the driveway and three rough-looking young men ambled up to the door. With a puzzled expression, Walter invited them in. The three made their business brief. After some mumbled remarks to Walter, one of them pulled out some money and awkwardly thrust it into Vivian's hand. Then they trooped out the door.

Vivian's reaction was a story in itself. She looked at the money, whispered, "Praise the Lord!" and pushed one of the bills toward us. "Here, this is for you," she said. "The Lord sent it."

Just then, Walter came back, holding two more bills. "Here's some more money they gave me," he said.

Vivian excitedly jumped up. "There's one for you and one for us," she exclaimed, thrusting another bill in our direction.

Her explanation brought wonder and praise. After the previous night's meeting, Vivian felt deeply burdened because she had nothing to give to us. She discussed the problem with Walter. They had no money whatever. So Vivian said, "If God sends us some money in the morning, may I give part of it to the missionaries?" Walter had been quick to agree, but doubted that even the Almighty could produce funds on such short notice.

Before going to bed, Vivian committed the matter to the Lord. All morning she had waited to see how He would answer, but the appearance of the three men still came as a surprise. They had been involved in an accident with her husband's motorcycle and had agreed to pay the damages; after nine months, however, Walter had despaired of getting anything. Their arrival that morning was a direct answer to Vivian's prayer.

It was a lesson in faith that I'm sure Walter and Vivian will not soon forget. Neither will we.

—Robert Erny/Indonesia

WEEK 2/MONDAY

THE GATES SHALL NOT BE SHUT

Thus saith the LORD, . . . I will loose the loins of kings, to open before him the two leaved gates; and the gates shall not be shut (Isa. 45:1 KJV).

For almost two years, no visas had been granted for new missionaries to Colombia. All possible legal steps had been taken to obtain their entry, but to no avail. On one occasion, a government official gave verbal approval, but the final consent via cable never came. We knew that no further visas could be expected without a miracle, and many Christians were praying for that miracle.

Bruce Hess, our Colombian field director, desperately needed to obtain five visas. He had been granted three personal interviews with the Office of Foreign Relations; six times he had talked with the chief of their visa department. At last, the official agreed to grant the visas that had been pending for so long.

Bruce went to pick them up, only to be told, "The papers cannot be found." He was told to return in an hour. Then he was put off until the next day.

On his knees in prayer that night, Bruce gained the assurance that the visas would be obtained. God called to mind the promise of Philippians 4:6–7: "Do not be anxious about anything, but in everything, by prayer and petition, with thanksgiving, present your requests to God. And the peace of God, which transcends all understanding, will guard your hearts and your minds in Christ Jesus."

Bruce returned to the visa department the next morning. Yes, he was told, the visa papers had been located. "But the cable will not go out for two days," the secretary said.

25

Bruce wondered, *Did the officials intend to withhold approval again, despite this verbal promise?* Perhaps.

The day for the cable arrived. It was no coincidence that, in a printed prayer guide for missions, Christians around the world were asked to pray for missionaries to Colombia that day. Thousands of prayers ascended to heaven on the missionaries' behalf, and the prayers prevailed. The confirming cables were sent on schedule.

Like Moses, we learn that God may send us to earthly authorities to demand, "Let My people go." We do not know why we sometimes encounter delays in receiving an answer. But God's promises are ours, and they cannot be broken.

—Mildred Young/Colombia

WEEK 2/TUESDAY

THE SURVIVAL KIT

Pray for us that the message of the Lord may spread rapidly and be honored. . . . And pray that we may be delivered from . . . evil men (2 Thess. 3:1–2).

On a cold, rainy afternoon in Quito, Ecuador, we assembled with other missionaries for a series of field council meetings. We craved the spiritual nourishment that our guest speaker, Dr. Ed Kilbourne, would bring.

Midway through the opening service, one of our children ran in and shouted, "Brock fell into the lake! Come quick!"

Fear pumped through my veins as I hurried to the dock. There stood our four-year-old Brock, cold and soaked, but safe. While I changed him into dry clothing, the story unfolded.

Walking along the dock with the other children, Brock had leaned over the water to snatch a piece of floating wood. He lost his balance and tumbled headfirst into the lake. Neither he nor anyone in the group could swim. But an Ecuadorian boy saw what was happening, dove into the water, and rescued him.

We were shaken, but jubilant about the way God had protected little Brock.

Eighteen months later, while I was home on furlough, a friend in our home church told me her story. One night she was awakened at midnight by a voice crying, "It's Brock! It's Brock! They just pulled him from a pool!" She sensed an urgent need to pray for our son. After about three hours, the Lord lifted this burden from her, and she returned to sleep.

While she was praying, it was 1:00 A.M. in Quito. Twelve hours later, our Brock was pulled from the lake.

My husband Willard recalls another occasion when a Christian "back home" interceded during an emergency. He was holding his first open-air meeting. While setting up the loudspeaker equipment atop a truck, he was seized with an almost overpowering fear that he would be stoned by the gathering crowd. He could not stop to pray, but in a moment the fear left him. Peace flooded into his heart. No harm came to him.

He related this experience at a mission convention in Calgary and saw a farmer in the audience beaming with joy. Before we left for Ecuador, this man had asked Willard for one of his prayer cards. One day rainy weather kept the farmer from working his land, so he took the opportunity to catch up on his bookkeeping. As he sifted through the papers on his desk, he found the prayer card. Gripped with a sudden desire to pray for us, he stopped his other work and interceded urgently for Willard. He could not recall the exact time and date; but the farmer was convinced it was another instance of "emergency praying."

Most Christians believe in the importance of prayer. But missionaries survive by it.

—Joan Hochhalter/Ecuador

WEEK 2/WEDNESDAY

A DIFFERENT WORLD

My grace is sufficient for you, for my power is made perfect in weakness (2 Cor. 12:9).

I expected adjustments during missionary service, and there had been a few in the thirty years since Bill and I, with our two-year-old Judy and baby Linda, began living in Colombia. But now, as a widow and a "seasoned" missionary already acquainted with the Spanish language, I thought life in modern Spain would be a breeze.

On the first morning in my new home, I tried to plug in an iron. It wouldn't go into the wall socket without an adapter. Then a transformer was needed to change the current to suit my American appliance. Even then, I learned, appliances with an electric motor (such as a mixer) will burn out. My electric alarm clock gained half an hour in a short time, so I nestled it away in storage.

Soon after I arrived in Madrid, I began searching for a badly needed fan. The price was 800 pesetas. *Let's see, 800 divided by 56.65. . . . Oh well,* I thought, *whatever it costs, it's not too much when the weather is this hot!* But it hardly measured up to the air conditioner I'd left in my apartment in the United States.

Buying a refrigerator posed another problem. Did my tiny kitchen have space for it? The only space measured 60 inches wide, and the refrigerator was 161 centimeters. *Well,* I thought, *if it doesn't fit, there's always the hallway*—which is where it stands, three-quarters of an inch too wide for the kitchen spot.

Although I have driven a car most of my life, driving in Madrid frightened me. Streets here aren't laid out in straight lines; they curve from one plaza to another. A street has one name for a distance, then suddenly changes to another.

Perhaps the most traumatic adjustment has been with my assignment as the mission's bookkeeper. Writing checks in Spanish, plus keeping four bank accounts (two in dollars and two in pesetas), has often driven me to prayer.

The adjustments will continue. But I am confident of being able to deal with them when I realize that Jesus Christ, who stepped from the perfection of heaven into this chaotic world, knows how to carry me over the hurdles of learning to live in a new environment.

—Mary Gillam/Spain

WEEK 2/THURSDAY

A MOMENT'S NOTICE

*You will keep in perfect peace him whose mind is steadfast, because he trusts in you. . . . Yes, L*ORD*, walking in the way of your laws, we wait for you; your name and renown are the desire of our hearts (Isa. 26:3, 8).*

It happened so suddenly! A voice on the phone spilled the news that our son Murray had been in a serious auto crash. An ambulance was rushing him from one hospital in Indianapolis to a better-equipped trauma center.

"Yes, we'll be there immediately," I stammered.

When we arrived, we found that small cuts covered Murray's neck, face, and chest; one large gash came dangerously close to his eye. X-rays confirmed the doctor's fears that most of the bones in Murray's face had been broken. A broken bone had ruptured the membrane covering the front of his brain, and spinal fluid was draining out. His left wrist was crushed and two fingers mangled.

Murray seemed oblivious to those around him, but he responded at times to the questions of his attendants. A nurse asked him twice, "Murray, where are you?"

Both times, he answered, "I'm on the altar."

We did not know the full import of that unconscious reply. Though the doctors did a fine job of repairing Murray's wounds, they confessed, "We're not sure he can make it."

Nearly a week passed before Murray's mind cleared. (He still does not remember the accident or anything of the first days afterward.) Yet marvelous healing began immediately. The doctors were amazed and predicted that he could be released in six weeks; but two weeks later, Murray went home to recuperate.

We do not know why this sudden crisis came to our lives. But through the long hours of waiting, the power of God was sufficient, and that lesson was precious in itself.

—Wayne Kenyon/Ecuador

PRAYER HOTLINE

Pray in the Spirit on all occasions with all kinds of prayers and requests. With this in mind, be alert and always keep on praying for all the saints (Eph. 6:18).

My husband Rolland and I were missionaries in Asia for over thirty years. The beginning of World War II ousted us from China, but we returned to Peking in 1946. We made the return trip on a converted troop transport ship that hadn't been greatly converted. Twenty-four women and children swarmed over a cabin that was four decks below the surface of the water, and we ate at long tables with benches, as had the troops before us.

One day we heard a loud commotion on the top deck. Rushing up the stairs, we found our captain standing at the bow, pointing to a round object in the water, about twenty feet from the ship. It was a mine left from the war, a menace that threatened to dispatch all of us.

We thanked the Lord for protecting us from this grave danger, and we knew someone must have been praying for us. Weeks later, we learned of the experience of Dr. C. P. Culver, a director of our mission, which shed light on our narrowly averted disaster.

Dr. Culver had been at home in Winona Lake, Indiana, emptying some trash into his furnace. Just as he prepared to dump the mass of scrap paper into the flames, he caught a glimpse of our family—Rolland, our two children, and me—sinking beneath ocean waves and calling for help. He dropped his trash basket, fell to his knees on the basement floor, and began praying for our deliverance. As we checked the time of his experience, we found that it was exactly the hour we had passed so close to the sea mine.

Prayer is the Christian's hotline to heaven. In answer to prayer, our all-powerful God can exert His influence anywhere.

—Mildred Rice/Taiwan

WEEK 2/SATURDAY

A TIME FOR EVERYTHING

There is a time for everything ... a time to search and a time to give up (Eccl. 3:1, 6).

When February came, I started to have the frantic feeling that usually signals the approach of furlough time. No one was available to take over teaching my English Bible class, and my Japanese co-worker was to be married and move away in March. Only three Friday meetings remained before we would have to stop holding the class. I wondered what would happen to ladies in the group like Mrs. Kato, who had not yet accepted Christ.

Many times I had jostled through crowds of Japanese people and felt the enormity of our task—imagine trying to reach 120 million people with the gospel! Ours was only a small group of women; but I felt overwhelmed by the task of reaching even them.

Our next Bible lesson concerned the dying thief on the cross. I explained that the thief had time only to repent of his sins and believe in Jesus Christ; he had no time to study Scripture or do good works. Mrs. Kato heaved a great sigh of relief. "I'm so glad to know that all I have to do is repent and believe," she said. A few hours later, she put her trust in Jesus.

Her conversion became a double cause for rejoicing. Every woman in the class now had either accepted Christ or had begun attending church services regularly. It seemed as though God was saying, "Judy, I did not intend for the burden I gave you to become burdensome. It's time for you to relinquish the class. My work here does not depend upon you."

God may grip us with concern for the spiritual plight of

a nation, or for a few individuals. But He knows we cannot endure the continuing weight of personal responsibility for every unsaved person we meet. So He changes our prayer duties from time to time; He releases us from our burdens. This release does not indicate coldness on our part; God simply calls us to begin dealing with someone else.

And when He calls us to relinquish a prayer burden He has placed upon us, we can be sure that He will continue to work in the lives of those to whom we have given ourselves in prayer and ministry.

—Judy Amos/Japan

WEEK 3/SUNDAY

ANGELS STANDING BY

*He will call upon me, and I will answer him; I will be
with him in trouble, I will deliver him and honor him
(Ps. 91:15).*

"Hey! What do you think you're doing?"

I heard my husband's voice shouting. Then came
sounds of a sudden scramble down the stairs as Ed
chased the early morning intruder out the window through
which he had gained entrance. It had been a rude
awakening to turn over at two in the morning and find a
robber standing at the foot of our bed!

Our frustration and shock mounted as we discovered
that he had taken most of our electrical appliances, plus
my husband's briefcase, full of important documents.

The noise had aroused our fellow missionaries and
neighbors, who came to see what was happening. After the
police came, we paused to thank God for sparing our lives.
What a beautiful hour that was for a prayer meeting!

At the same hour, the Holy Spirit woke Ed's mother in
Wisconsin. Through a dream, He impressed on her that we
needed help. So she too joined us in that prayer meeting,
though separated by thousands of miles.

It was only our third night in Costa Rica, where we had
come to take language classes. But the Lord had other
lessons for us to learn. He proved His word in Psalm 91:
"For he will command his angels concerning you to guard
you in all your ways" (v. 11). How can we ever doubt His
love for us?   —Carol Anderson/Colombia

WEEK 3/MONDAY

ALONE, ILL, AND AFRAID

Do not be anxious about anything, but in everything, by prayer and petition, with thanksgiving, present your requests to God. And the peace of God, which transcends all understanding, will guard your hearts and your minds in Christ Jesus (Phil. 4:6–7).

You may think that missionaries easily conquer the spiritual problems that assail ordinary Christians, vanquishing the "little foxes that spoil the vines" of other followers of the Lord—worry, ill health, frustration, and doubt. Well, don't believe it! I am living proof of a missionary who worried and fretted under the power of doubt.

Over forty years ago, I went to serve in China. War drove us out, but we went to Taiwan in the 1950s. Later, my husband died. So I knew the testing of personal danger, death, and grief. But I was unprepared for the spiritual devastation that an incurable illness wreaked upon me.

Over six years ago, doctors told me that I have an incurable liver ailment and a serious lung disorder. They arrived at their diagnosis after exhaustive—and exhausting—batteries of tests. (Perhaps you know the sudden pain that comes when a medical technician unexpectedly strikes a disagreeable spot in your body. Perhaps you have felt the uncertainty that grows as a result of those mysterious and unfamiliar sensations.)

Sickness is a serious matter for the person living alone. I lay night after night, dreading the onset of a surprise attack upon my body. Without warning, I would be seized by a terrifying chill. For perhaps two hours at a stretch, my teeth would chatter violently, and my bed would shake with the tremors of my body. Then, as abruptly as it came, the attack would leave—and I would lie totally exhausted, wasted and afraid.

At other times, my breath became so short that I hardly dared to move. Taking ten steps would wear me out, and I would fall into a chair to rest.

One day, the warming sun and spring breeze lured me into my yard, all asplash with flowers. There I tripped and fell, which proved to be a calamity, for I sustained a compressed fracture of a vertebra. How could I get back into the house to reach the phone? Pain devoured me as I crawled up the steps.

Again and again, I have floundered in my physical ailments. But I know beyond all doubt that I am in God's care. The "very present help" is aware of my need those lonely nights I lay quivering like an aspen leaf.

Some spiritual lessons are learned only in darkness. So I have come to depend solely upon God as a result of my personal need. As a missionary, I may have said a thousand times that God alone was my strength and salvation; but now I realize what that truly means.

—Edna Chandler/Taiwan

WEEK 3/TUESDAY

HANDS AROUND THE WORLD

Join me in my struggle by praying to God for me (Rom. 15:30).

For weeks, our five-year-old Kushi had nursed a neighbor's sick dog. Then we heard that the neighbor had died of rabies contracted from the dog.

Rabies can be spread without a bite; an infected dog's lick on a small cut or abrasion will do it. So great fear crammed a solid rock into the pit of my stomach. While trying to pour coffee for breakfast guests, I was so upset that I spilled the whole pot.

An American pediatrician advised that Kushi immediately receive shots of vaccine. Finding that our doctor in Madras had none, we began a frantic search. The American Embassy had a small supply of vaccine, but it was available only for diplomatic personnel. Sensing our great need, we called our home church in California to request prayer; within hours, about four thousand people were interceding for us.

A nurse at the American Embassy referred us to another doctor in our city who had the vaccine. He looked at Kushi's hands, covered with scratches, and immediately started her on the injections. But he expected us to replace the vaccine, which seemed impossible. In the midst of this crisis, a friend from Delhi paid an unexpected visit. With her was a woman whom we had not met—the head nurse of the American Consulate hospital. Hearing our story, the nurse arranged to replace the doctor's supply at no cost to us.

Kushi escaped rabies. We thanked our friends back home who enfolded us in prayer when we ourselves could not pray adequately.

On my first tour of missionary duty, I had sensed keenly the lack of prayer support by people back home. But on our first furlough, we made contact with a church of praying friends. That congregation has consistently kept close to us with newsletters, tapes of the pastor's sermons, and letters expressing personal interest in us. More important, these co-workers in the States add their continuing prayer support, so vital to our success on the mission field.

—Carol Houghton/India

WEEK 3/WEDNESDAY

WHEN THE MUSIC STOPS

I will extol the LORD at all times. . . . let the afflicted hear and rejoice. Glorify the LORD with me; let us exalt his name together (Ps. 34:1–3).

"Da-da-DUM! Da-da-DUM!"

The bongo drum pounded out that rhythm for the umpteenth time as the throbbing in my head kept time. Five nights a week, from eleven to three, the pulsating beat from the Mariachi Night Club boomed into our apartment. I like music; but the incessant guitars, trumpets—and, worst of all, the drums—destroyed my composure. There was no escape.

For weeks, I suffered . . . and complained. Then a fellow missionary spoke in a prayer meeting about "counting it all joy" in difficult situations. She referred to Joni Eareckson's book, *A Step Further.* Strapped down in her Stryker frame for two weeks, Joni could do nothing but stare at the floor. To make it worse, she managed to get the Hong Kong flu while in that position. "Why, Lord? Haven't I had enough?" she groaned.

My thoughts turned to the Latin music. I did not want to endure it. But, just as the Lord taught Joni to keep her eyes on Him during her suffering, He might be doing the same with me.

I had already discussed with several friends my problem of sleepless nights. I felt reassured when some agreed that I should not have to endure it. After all, who could possibly "count it all joy"?

But the comments of my missionary friend pointed me heavenward. I had been living too long on the earthly plane, seeking listeners and pity for my sad tale. Would I continue to do that? Or would I let God remove my cloak of self-pity and teach me joy?

I have learned that joy does come, not just "in the morning"—or when the music stops—but when my mind is filled with the One who created it.

—Kathy Coon/Ecuador

WEEK 3/THURSDAY

LINKED TO SUPREMACY

He is before all things, and in him all things hold together. And he is the head of the body, the church; he is the beginning and the firstborn from among the dead, so that in everything he might have the supremacy (Col. 1:17–18).

Time was running out. Less than a minute to go and still no score. Both teams skillfully maneuvered the ball; their strategies and reactions were almost flawless. In one last desperate effort, the team in blue jerseys drove the ball through the mass of red-jerseyed defenders. Almost like magic, the ball whizzed past the goalie into the waiting net. Amid thunderous cheers, the whistle sounded. The game was over. In a test of supremacy, the new world-champion soccer team had emerged.

Every day, tests of supremacy face us on a more serious level. Temptations, inner spiritual conflicts, even the goading little trials that test our patience will test our recognition of the supremacy of Christ—His supremacy in the world and His supremacy in our lives. The struggle against His supremacy has been underway since Satan spearheaded his rebellion against the Godhead.

However, God anticipated this struggle and dealt with it long before it arose. Thus, Paul wrote to the Colossians that Christ is "the firstborn from among the dead, so that in everything he might have the supremacy" (v. 18). Christ is already supreme. The struggle continues only because His creation refuses to yield to His supremacy.

The apostle Paul further states that this struggle "is not against flesh and blood, but . . . against the powers of this dark world and against the spiritual forces of evil in the heavenly realms" (Eph. 6:12). The challenger to Christ's supremacy presses his fight, and his attack will not cease until the end of time.

Our strategy in this conflict must be a strong defense. "Put on the full armor of God so that you can take your stand against the devil's schemes," Paul says (Eph. 6:11). Even our armor suggests that we are to take the stance of defense: the belt of truth, the breastplate of righteousness, the foot armor of readiness, the shield of faith, and the helmet of salvation. Our only offensive weapon for the contest is the sword of the Spirit, which is the Word of God. And we are to wield it with the spirit of a champion.

The world struggles to resist the supremacy of Christ. And because we are linked to His supremacy, the world often struggles against us. But we have a sure defense against the efforts of our adversary.

—Wesley Wildermuth/Indonesia

WEEK 3/FRIDAY

FILLED WITH THE SPIRIT

Do not be foolish, but understand what the Lord's will is. Do not get drunk on wine, which leads to debauchery. Instead, be filled with the Spirit (Eph. 5:17-18).

Our Lord believed that the presence of the Holy Spirit was essential to the success of His work and the fulfillment of His commission. Without the Holy Spirit, Christ's disciples could only remain a timorous, divided band of men destined for obscurity. But when He possessed them, they became an invincible church.

By today's standards, that small apostolic band was underfinanced, pitifully equipped, and greatly disorganized for its task. Yet within thirty years the apostles had carried the gospel throughout the then-known world. How did they do it?

Samuel Chadwick tells us: "Pentecost turned anemic believers into exuberant saints. People said they were drunk, and so they were, but not with wine. They were vivacious and abounding with vitality. Pentecost wakes people up. It vitalizes talent and makes the utmost of every faculty and gift."

We have grieved the Holy Spirit by trying to do God's work without Him. It is high time to acknowledge our sin.

Without the Holy Spirit, our most earnest endeavor for Christ is play-acting. Human wisdom, even the most prudent administrative procedures, will fail without Him. In our spiritual warfare, the only effective weapons are spiritual ones—weapons fashioned by the Holy Spirit and wielded by Spirit-filled people.   —Eugene A. Erny/India

WEEK 3/SATURDAY

OUR BEST CONTACT

The Lord will guide you always (Isa. 58:11).

"Lord, lead us to the place You have prepared." That had been our prayer for many months. Our Japan field director had written to mission leaders in the Kinki District, asking for leads on housing. Nothing. We called friends there. Nothing. With time getting short, Chuck and I decided to scout the area ourselves.

Since our assignment was to work with the thirteen churches of the district and assist in starting new ones, we needed a central location. Nishinomiya City seemed the best. During a random drive through the streets, we emerged from a narrow side street onto a wide four-lane thoroughfare. Turning left, we found ourselves in front of the Shukugawa train station. Across the street was a rental agency.

The agent showed us floor plans for three houses. One was far too small; another would be too noisy. But the last house was just a few minutes from the station, so we asked to see it.

Walking up the stone steps to the house, we saw workmen. "Oh, there is one thing I should tell you," the agent said. "This house is being completely refurbished and won't be available until July 1." Exactly the date we wanted occupancy!

Chuck and I checked off our list of needs: long-term rental (the owner had no other plan for the house), close to transportation (within minutes of three train lines), close to shopping (neighborhood stores within a block), a good-sized kitchen (one of the largest I have seen in a Japanese home), a study for Chuck (the perfect place upstairs), a guest room (with space for six tatami mats), a garage (underneath the small front yard), and privacy.

Yet this was the first house we had seen, just minutes after arriving in town. We shouldn't take the *first* house we saw, should we? But other rental agencies had none available, so we made final arrangements to rent the house that same day.

Our friend, Mr. Sengoku, exclaimed, "But that is impossible!" Even Japanese people with extensive personal contacts found it difficult to secure adequate housing. And many landlords were reluctant to rent to non-Japanese.

We knew, of course, that our personal Contact—a loving heavenly Father—topped all the others!

—JoAnn Dupree/Japan

THREE STEPS TO POWER

Far be it from me that I should sin against the LORD
by failing to pray for you (1 Sam. 12:23).

Every Christian believes in prayer, but few have power
in prayer. Do you? I have found that we must pay a price to
obtain prevailing power in our prayer for others:

1. *A life filled with the Holy Spirit.* The born-again
child of God must make a total surrender to God, ask in
faith for the Holy Spirit, and receive the initial filling of the
Spirit. But then the Spirit-filled Christian must be filled
again and again. How? By daily thirsting for more of the
Spirit, rejoicing in more of the Spirit, and obeying God in
constant loving acts of obedience. He always gives His
Spirit to those who ask and obey.

Few people keep so full of the Holy Spirit that rivers of
life-giving water flow from within them (see John 7:37–39).
Ask yourself whether anything keeps you from being
flooded again and again by fresh outpourings of the Holy
Spirit. The more Spirit-filled you are, the more easily the
Holy Spirit can empower your prayers.

2. *Time in prayer.* You cannot become effective in
prayer unless you are willing to take the time. If you spend
only a few minutes in prayer morning and evening, and if
you seldom read more than a chapter of the Bible each
day, you cannot expect to be anything but a "prayer baby."

Serious prayer takes time. Don't fool yourself. You can
find the time for earnest intercessory prayer if you really
want to. You find time to do all of the things you feel are
most important.

3. *Intercession for others.* You will never learn to pray
effectively as long as you spend most of your prayers on

yourself and your loved ones. You are to be a priest for others to God (1 Peter 2:5, 9). God will not greatly honor the prayer of any Christian whose prayer life is self-centered.

Ask God to guide you in preparing and using prayer lists. Begin to pray specifically for the needs of others. Pray for fellow Christians, your pastor, other spiritual leaders, national leaders, and God's work in other countries. Name missionaries and pray for them in loving detail.

Every Christian can become strong in prayer. Only three things are required: a Spirit-filled life, adequate time, and intercession for others. Is this more than you are willing to pay?

—Wesley L. Duewel/India

WEEK 4/MONDAY

FAITH LIKE DANIEL'S

Jesus Christ is the same yesterday and today and forever (Heb. 13:8).

The young son of Pastor Saito had been hospitalized for four months and was declining. With blood vessels becoming blocked and breaking under the skin, his body was covered with bruises. Added to that, he had nephritis, a grave kidney disorder. The doctor announced his grim prognosis to the parents: "No hope."

But after earnest prayer and the laying on of hands, the boy rallied from the coma that had lasted for weeks. Daily gaining energy and strength, he was soon able to leave the hospital on weekends to be with his family and to attend church services. "It is near to a resurrection!" his father exclaimed.

Our God is the same as Daniel's. Our impossibilities can become God's opportunities to work miracles, as in the day of that great Old Testament prophet.

Daniel was rescued from the jaws of death because of his faith in the Lord. "No wound was found on him, because he had trusted in his God" (Dan. 6:23). "My God sent his angel, and he shut the mouths of the lions. They have not hurt me," Daniel announced to the king (v. 22).

Daniel's faithful prayer life serves as an example for us. Coupled with his prayer was an obvious, unwavering faith in God. And God rewards the faith of His servants. Just ask Pastor Saito.

—Art Shelton/Japan

WEEK 4/TUESDAY

OF WORMS AND KINGS

You are no longer a slave, but a son; and since you are a son, God has made you also an heir (Gal. 4:7).

In the wee Michigan village where I grew up, we used to play a game called "king of the mountain." The object was to attain the summit of a dirt pile and then keep everyone else off. It required a great deal of running and leaping about to keep one's position secure.

Christians are potential kings—but some never seem to realize their potential. They never rule. They never quite make it. They are always just outside what God would do with them. The result is that they have, not only a sense of frustration, but a sense of inferiority. They suppose they are nothing in God's scheme of things, of no use to God at all, and they are afraid to try becoming useful.

Isaac Watts surely was not conscious of Psalm 8 when he penned the lines, "Would He devote that sacred head / for such a worm as I?" Wormhood is not God's plan for His people. He expects us to *reign* as children of God. To be created a little lower than God (Ps. 8:5) does not imply any wormliness.

Paul tells us that "the whole creation is on tiptoe to see the wonderful sight of the sons of God coming into their own" (Rom. 8:19 PHILLIPS). Among other things, he means that we are not fully effective in claiming territory for the King of kings until we believe in ourselves.

Count Nicholas von Zinzendorf used to tell his Moravians, "Our Lamb has conquered; let us follow." Like Paul, he believed he could "do all things through Christ" (Phil. 4:13).

Note that the apostle did not say Christ could do all

things through Paul; he said that Paul himself could do them through Christ. God expects us to burst out of our shackled selves into "the glorious freedom of the children of God" (Rom. 8:21).

—Robert D. Wood/United States

WEEK 4/WEDNESDAY

MANHOLES

Each of us will give an account of himself to God. . . . Make up your mind not to put any stumbling block or obstacle in your brother's way (Rom. 14:12–13).

Early one morning as I walked the streets of Bogota, I stopped short of an open manhole. I nearly fell into it!

Curiosity prompted me to peer inside. At a depth of several feet, on top of rusted pipes, two street lads had curled up to sleep. I yearned to give those homeless boys a better bed. I envisioned that they might be swept away by swirling floodwaters or become the victims of poisonous gas.

Open manholes can result in tragedy. Why are such dangers left unguarded? Perhaps because of forgetfulness, carelessness, or a simple lack of concern for others.

Reflecting on the incident, I began to realize that the finger of accusation pointed my way. How often had my careless living, my forgetfulness, and my cool concern for others left an open pit for them? How many new or weak Christians had stumbled into a yawning trap that I had left by my unconcern or neglect?

I recall the time when I impulsively passed on a juicy morsel of gossip. How it grew! And people were hurt. I had left an open manhole that could be closed only by my repenting before God and asking forgiveness of those I had harmed. Perhaps others had fallen into the practice of gossip because of me. They may have said, "If she can do it, I can too."

Jesus said, "If anyone causes one of these little ones who believe in me to sin, it would be better for him to have a large millstone hung around his neck and to be drowned in the depths of the sea" (Matt. 18:6). Jesus considers it serious business when we leave open manholes.

—Florence Cavender/Colombia

WEEK 4/THURSDAY

WEATHER, OR NO

The eyes of the Lord are everywhere, keeping watch on the wicked and the good (Prov. 15:3).

While we finished breakfast, my husband picked up the Bible and a book of stories about everyday life. He began reading about a little girl who was upset with God. She had prayed for sunshine for the picnic day but, as she looked outside, rain poured. Her mother explained that God knows best what we need. The little girl agreed, but had no smile as she pressed her nose against the window pane.

Breakfast and prayer time finished, our three boys dashed off to school. The story seemed forgotten in our activities of the day.

That evening, five-year-old Stevie began his prayers with, "Thank you, Jesus for the fun times I had today." (I thought, *How many times I forget to thank Him for the "fun times"!*) "Tomorrow help Johnny not to hit me—and help me not to hit him back." (*Sometimes I even forget to ask for God's help in the hard places of life.*) "Help me not to leave my marbles in the hall where Mommy might trip and break her leg." (That sounded like a direct quote from me! But I wondered, *Do I really care about other people?*)

Stevie was just beginning to say amen when he paused and added, "Oh, by the way, Jesus—any kind of weather is all right with me."

The story we had read that morning flashed to mind, and I smiled as I pulled the covers up to Stevie's chin. My smile withered, though, as I left Stevie's room. Suddenly, I realized the difference between our prayers. He was really saying, "You make the decisions, Lord. I'll take cheerfully whatever You send my way." I did not have faith to pray that way.

In my room, I began to talk with God. Life's weather had been rough recently; I had complained and even rebeled. I could see no need for things to be the way they were. Now, through my son, God had shown a better way. He wanted to be my strength, my security and peace through the storms. And He promised to be near to guide me in the sunshine.

"All right, Lord," I prayed simply. "I'll take hands off. You give me what You know is best. I'll trust You. And any kind of weather is all right with me."

—Bette Crouse/Korea

WEEK 4/FRIDAY

NO SMALL VOICE

Without faith it is impossible to please God, because anyone who comes to him must believe that he exists and that he rewards those who earnestly seek him (Heb. 11:6).

Would God heal me? I was a long way from home and suffering with severe pain. Desperate for relief, I had seen a doctor earlier that day.

The clinic diagnosed a structural problem in my back, possibly resulting from an earlier fall. To complicate that, I was riding for long hours, carrying heavy luggage and boxes of literature, and sleeping on soft beds.

However, I believed that God wanted me to continue this tour of leading prayer conferences, so I prayed that He would show me what to do. Others prayed with me for healing, and I wondered whether God would heal me. But no "still small voice" provided the answer.

After breakfast, my colleague Vi Haines talked with me about an experience she'd had the night before. As she prayed before retiring, God prompted her to read the story of a woman who touched the edge of Jesus' cloak and was healed (Matt. 9:20–22). Vi felt that Scripture affirmed God's desire to heal me.

Funny—I was the one who had prayed for guidance. But God gave it to Vi for me!

Together we read the Scripture passage. I explained to God that I could not honestly say that I had enough faith to be healed. However, I offered Him all the faith I had and asked Him to add sufficient faith to make healing possible.

The next few days brought no change in my condition, but Vi and I continued to give thanks to God and hold our ground. My traveling partner for the next meeting arrived. Secretly, I wondered if I could go.

Then I recalled the story of Jesus and the ten lepers. "As they went, they were cleansed," the Bible said (Luke 17:14). So I decided to go to the next meeting, in faith that I would be healed.

While riding in the car, I suddenly realized that I was free from pain. Jesus had healed my back, head, legs, and other affected areas. It was a complete healing.

I believe it was significant that God led my sensitive friend to form a needed partnership of prayer and faith with me. I did not need to place faith in my own faith. Healing does not result from the greatness or smallness of our faith, but from *the faithfulness of God to answer.*

—Alice Huff/United States

WEEK 4/SATURDAY

KEEP YOUR PLACE

I meditate on your precepts and consider your ways. I delight in your decrees; I will not neglect your word (Ps. 119:15–16).

Some Indonesians believe the *place* where one prays is very important. The folk writer Giman tells of spending three days and nights in a hole in the ground, seeking God's will for his future. On another occasion, a holy man hollowed out a tree trunk to provide a place for meditation and prayer. (When he was finished, no one dared to cut it into planks because they considered it too sacred.)

In the New Testament, we find Christ praying in a garden, on a public street, in people's homes, in the temple, in the Upper Room, and on the cross. His favorite spot for prayer, however, was on a mountaintop. Though He could call on the resources of heaven at any time, in any place or circumstance, He often chose nights or early mornings for uninterrupted prayer on a mountain.

How can we find such a secluded place for prayer? It's usually impossible for us to go physically to a mountaintop; but isn't there some mountain of communion with God for every one of us?

A mountain represents separation from the world and its distractions. Each of us should seek places that can be "holy mountains" for our daily conversations with God. This may require a family conference, to determine a time and place in which other family members will honor our privacy. But the rewards will be well worth any effort needed to guard these times alone with the Lord.

Jesus said, "When you pray, go into your room, close the door and pray to your Father, who is unseen. Then your

Father, who sees what is done in secret, will reward you" (Matt. 6:6). Each of us must find a place of seclusion to commune with Him.

—Nancy Gill/Indonesia

WEEK 5/SUNDAY

DATE ON A HONDA

Before they call I will answer; while they are still speaking I will hear (Isa. 65:24).

Mile after mile, I struggled with the cargo of electronic equipment strapped to my motorcycle. Without doubt, the road was one of the worst I had traveled in Haiti. My destination was Don Don, a town nestled among the mountains. But as the route grew more dangerous and exhausting, I wondered whether I should continue.

Spurring me on was the clear-cut purpose of the venture. In order to plan our missionary radio strategy for reaching the interior of the country, we had to know the present strength of our radio signal there. My assignment was to carry a radio receiver into the mountains to test our reception.

Along the way, I dodged hundreds of Haitians who trekked the narrow trail with market wares balanced on their heads. They impeded my progress and demanded careful driving.

At one point, donkeys loaded with fruit and charcoal wedged me off the path. A rut well over a foot deep trapped the Honda's wheels, hurling me to the ground. Shaken, I righted my bike. To my surprise, a bruised knee was the only injury.

I could not have had a warmer welcome at my destination. Advance announcements over Radio 4VEH had prepared the people of Don Don for my visit. Hundreds gathered around me; the police also arrived to keep back the crowd and silence their blaring radios so I could concentrate.

My work completed, I mounted the Honda for the

three-and-a-half-hour return journey. At home, I sank into a chair to reflect on the Lord's care during the day. Why wasn't my equipment damaged when the cycle flipped over? What kept me from tumbling down the mountain, time and again?

I glanced at our missionary prayer calendar. Drawing it closer, I saw that our family was featured for prayer that very day. How tremendous! I wondered whether those who prayed for us could have realized the important role they played in our lives that day.

—Claude Beachy/Haiti

WEEK 5/MONDAY

WHEN GOD STEPPED IN

If my people, who are called by my name, will humble themselves and pray and seek my face and turn from their wicked ways, then will I hear from heaven and will forgive their sin and will heal their land (2 Chron. 7:14).

We were a restless group. We numbered twelve missionaries and two Chinese pastors teaching in the Bible school at Peking in the early 1930s. But there was no joy in our prayer meetings. We sensed a deep gulf between us and our Chinese co-workers. We decided there was only one way through the problem—prayer—so we agreed to fast and pray during the noon hour each day.

Our desperate prayers sounded like, "Lord, You know how much Pastor Chou needs Your help. And Pastor Wang is a thorn in the flesh to most of us. . . ." We expected God to work a miracle in our Chinese co-workers; but days passed and nothing happened.

Mercifully, God revealed the error in our thinking. Jealousy, pride of position, and lack of love had hindered us. As usual, faults are thick when love is thin.

Word got around that the American missionaries were confessing their sins and praying together. Eventually, our Chinese leaders were called into the noontime prayer meeting to hear our testimonies. Before long Pastor Chou broke in. "If our missionary brothers and sisters need this," he said, "what about us?"

Each of us sought forgiveness. Personal differences melted away and a loving oneness prevailed. Pastor Wang made a complete about-face and became our strongest friend.

In retrospect, we believe that was a special preparation for the war days that soon followed. Some of the Chinese students who shared in the revival were martyred for their faith. One who was flogged repeatedly was told that he would be spared further punishment if he would renounce his faith in Christ, but he would not.

Each of us involved in the Peking revival had to pay a price during the years that followed. The war years brought several evacuations and transfers to other countries, not an easy experience, even in peacetime. But we learned that we had new inner strength by walking in the Spirit daily.

God is ready to step into our lives and bring revival if we will humble ourselves and seek His face.

—Eugene and Esther Erny/China

WEEK 5/TUESDAY

THE BRANCH

A righteous man may have many troubles, but the
LORD *delivers him from them all; he protects [him] (Ps.*
34:19–20).

Scenes from the books of Jack London and Admiral
Byrd whirled through my mind. They had written about
"white-outs," when snow or fog cut travelers' visibility to
zero; surely we were in one.

With other Christian youth workers, I had traveled to
Switzerland for a brief vacation. The sun shone brightly
during our four days in the tiny Swiss towns. Encouraged
by the good weather, we decided to visit the small country
of Andorra en route home.

But as we curved up the mountain road, visibility
steadily faded. We knew that a great chasm stretched
alongside the road, and only wooden poles fifteen feet
apart marked the road's edge. At the height of the white-
out, we creeped along, straining to catch sight of those
posts that separated us from certain death. At times they
were barely discernible. But we never completely lost sight
of those sentinels of life.

Back safely in Madrid, I pondered a phrase in Zecha-
riah 6:12: "Here is the man whose name is the Branch."
This prophetic reference had always seemed vague to me;
but now it took on personal meaning. Life is confusing at
times, and my perception of God's way will fade. But like
the guardposts, He who is the Branch carefully guards my
path, even on the most treacherous climb.

—Debi Grout/Spain

WEEK 5/WEDNESDAY

LEARNING HIS LANGUAGE

Come near to God and he will come near to you (James 4:8).

Have you ever visited a country where you could not speak the people's language? Most missionaries face this situation. And they know that they must master the language of the country if they are to proclaim the gospel effectively there. This involves more than verbal communication; language involves the heart of a people and is expressed in all the subtle customs of everyday life.

The same is true of our relationship with God. If we are to hear and understand His voice, we must learn the way in which He communicates.

Jesus knew that the desires of His Father would be revealed only through prayer. Is it any wonder, then, that He lived prayerfully while on this earth? "Very early in the morning . . . Jesus got up, left the house and went off to a solitary place, where he prayed" (Mark 1:35). "After he had dismissed them, he went up into the hills by himself to pray" (Matt. 14:23). "Crowds of people came to hear him and to be healed of their sicknesses. But Jesus often withdrew to lonely places and prayed" (Luke 5:15–16).

In prayer the language of God's heart is made known. To learn that language, we must have constant encounters with Him through prayer. A human language is not learned overnight; how much more is this true of the language we are to speak throughout eternity.

—Jeannine Brabon/Spain

WEEK 5/THURSDAY

INSTANT ACCESS

Since we have been justified through faith, we have peace with God through our Lord Jesus Christ, through whom we have gained access by faith into this grace in which we now stand. And we rejoice in the hope of the glory of God (Rom. 5:1–2).

After my father-in-law's death, a friend wrote his biography. The head of the company publishing it invited us to a luncheon at the London Press Club. But when we arrived, an official at the door asked, "What authority do you have to enter?" Unable to convince him, we were sent back outside.

Soon a taxi pulled up to the curb and our host climbed out. The three of us approached the door and were immediately accepted. Our relationship to our host provided access.

The apostle Paul explains that Jesus Christ gives us immediate access to the heavenly Father. And our acceptance in Him provides access to all divine resources.

I saw an example of this while visiting with a farmer friend last year. Although very busy, he prays six hours a day—two in the morning, two at midday, and two in the evening. He's a radiant, humble, and effective Christian witness.

While I was there, he asked God to send someone to whom he could witness. He lives in an isolated area and seldom sees another soul. But that morning a salesman arrived.

"I have come to sell seed," the salesman announced.

"You haven't," my friend answered. "You're here because I asked God to send you today. Let's get back in your car so I can talk with you."

For the next hour, the farmer talked with him about Christ, then he called me to join them. The salesman was still unwilling to accept Christ. So my friend prayed, "Lord, I have taken an hour of this man's time. He should have been selling seed, and he hasn't sold any. Please make up to him the hour he has missed."

That evening the salesman returned to tell us he had done three times as much business as in a normal day. Looking at him, my friend said, "See how much God loves you and wants to save you?" Using his access rights, that farmer wrestles in prayer until people come to the Savior.

Thank God for access to His unlimited resources. Will you allow Him to dispense them for you today?

—Stanley Banks/England

WEEK 5/FRIDAY

JUST IN TIME

*The salvation of the righteous comes from the LORD;
he is their stronghold in time of trouble. The LORD helps
them and delivers them (Ps. 37:39–40).*

During the Japanese occupation of China, I met Mrs.
Wang, a widow with three children. Her employer had
treated her shamefully, with the result that she was
expecting a fourth child. Stunned by her predicament, she
considered suicide. Her cousin brought her to me. Mrs.
Wang begged me to hide her until the delivery of the baby.
Wartime circumstances made that impossible; but I urged
her to accept Christ as her Savior and allow Him to provide
a hiding place.

After I had made many visits with much prayer, Mrs.
Wang did so. Then God opened a door in answer to prayer:
A mission orphanage agreed to shelter her and keep the
baby, if I would pay for her food. Although she had been a
Christian for only a few weeks, Mrs. Wang knew this must
be God's provision.

Before we left for the orphanage, we read the Bible and
prayed together. As I went to call a rickshaw, she suddenly
became quite distressed; she couldn't find her identification card. While changing her gown, she had left it on
a table in her cousin's home.

My heart sank. It would be impossible to get past the
guards at the city gate without proof of her identity. Mrs.
Wang had to leave the city by three o'clock and it was
already fifteen minutes to three; but it would require an
hour to get to her cousin's house and back.

"But can't we pray?" she asked, as her face lit up.

I wasn't very hopeful as we knelt together again. But

while Mrs. Wang calmly asked her heavenly Father for help, we heard running feet stop outside our door. Her breathless cousin burst into the room. Waving the identification card, she gasped, "Am I too late? Am I too late?"

The cousin briefly related her story. On her way to do church visitation, she had been stopped by soldiers who asked to see her identification card. Suddenly, she wondered if Mrs. Wang had taken hers. Surely she had. But the nagging thought persisted so strongly that she went back home to check. There lay the card.

I could scarcely believe it. God had answered prayer before we discovered there was any need. Watching Mrs. Wang pass inspection at the gate, I repeated words that she probably had never heard: "Before they call I will answer; while they are still speaking I will hear" (Isa. 65:24).

—Annie Kartozian/Taiwan

WEEK 5/SATURDAY

MATTER-OF-FACT FAITH

Now faith is the assurance (the confirmation, the title-deed) of the things [we] hope for, being the proof of things [we] do not see and the conviction of their reality—faith perceiving as real fact what is not revealed to the senses (Heb. 11:1 AMP.).

She was just a little girl, about to enter first grade in the autumn. No, not just a little girl—she was a little girl with a large understanding of God.

Debbie's eye had been on Mrs. M., a deeply loving first-grade teacher. She wanted to be in her class. But Mrs. M. was to teach second grade that fall; in fact, she had cleared her classroom cupboards and taken her first-grade materials home.

But Debbie prayed all summer that Mrs. M. would be her teacher. To forestall disappointment, her parents kept reminding her that it could not be; Mrs. M. was to teach second grade. But Debbie's reply was always the same, "I know." She spoke it quietly, but matter-of-factly, as if she knew something the grownups didn't.

Two weeks before school opened, the principal changed his mind. He assigned Mrs. M. back to the first grade.

I have often thought of the matter-of-factness of Debbie's faith. The psalmist said that "the Lord is my shepherd; . . . I shall not lack" (Ps. 23:1 AMP.). Jesus tried to teach His followers that our heavenly Father *knows* that we have need of certain things, implying that if He knows, He surely will supply them.

But we are so slow to learn this simplicity of trust. We need the attitude of a child at home, who has no need to wonder at the things that untrusting people fuss about. "I know," spoken assuredly of the Lord's unfailing fulfillment of His promises—that is the best expression of faith that one can make.

Blaise Pascal spoke of it when he said, "The heart has its reasons which reason knows nothing of." And he went on to say, "We know the truth, not only by the reason, but by the heart."

—Robert D. Wood/United States

IF IT PLEASE HIM

When all kinds of trials and temptations crowd into your lives ... don't resent them as intruders, but welcome them as friends! Realise that they come to test your faith and to produce in you the quality of endurance. But let the process go on until that endurance is fully developed (James 1:2–4 PHILLIPS).

The trip had brought nothing but problems. Everything that could go wrong had. And it wasn't over yet. I sat in the special clearance section of the Sydney airport, reading a book of poetry to pass the time.

Looking up from the book, I could see through tears that my luggage was still going round and round on the turntable. Yet another airline official was gingerly making his way toward me.

All was well when my family saw me off at Bishop Airport in Flint, Michigan. Planes that had been grounded by fog for two days were flying again. So I began my return flight to Indonesia. Though I dislike traveling alone, I committed the long, wearisome trip into God's hands; but I was blissfully unaware of what lay ahead.

Chicago's O'Hare Airport was its usual chaotic self, made worse by adverse weather. We were an hour late taking off for San Francisco. Instead of our scheduled stop in Denver, we refueled in Las Vegas, a process that took over an hour. We taxied to the end of the runway, only to hear the captain's voice intone the sad news: "San Francisco is fogbound; we must return to the terminal." After waiting several hours there, we were put up overnight at the Sands Hotel.

The next day, after a ten-hour layover in San Francisco,

we were turned back at the boarding gate. Someone had failed to inform the crew that they had a flight to Honolulu that day. We took off over the Pacific two hours late.

I prayed fervently that we'd make up the lost time. If not, I could not connect with the flight to Indonesia. We arrived in Sydney just fifteen minutes before the plane left for Indonesia; but I had to go through customs again, so I missed the flight.

The airline officials told me I could leave the airport only if I had an ongoing flight or a visa for an Australian visit. I had neither. The next available flight would go through Singapore and cost two hundred dollars more. Grumbling and fuming, I determined to sit in the airport until the airlines found a better solution. That was when I picked up the little book I had tucked in my bag at the last minute. It was aptly titled *No Easy Road.* I read accounts of people who had lost homes, children, everything in the service of Christ—lost everything except a sense of God's love. I had lost nothing but time. I wept as I thought of my selfish attitude.

By this time the airline official reached me. I would have to stay in Sydney overnight, he explained kindly, but they had found a direct flight to Indonesia the next day at no additional cost. So the next day I flew to Bali and on to Surabaya. As I touched down for the last time, I thanked God for working things out so well.

Co-workers from the mission met me at the airport, and we laughed over my experiences on the two-hour jaunt to Malang—most of the way, that is. Their car broke down halfway home! But this time, I actually laughed.

—Marilyn Wykes/Indonesia

*Dick Eastman, *No Easy Road* (Grand Rapids: Baker, 1973).

WEEK 6/MONDAY

GOD OF EMERGENCIES

Hear my urgent cry. I will call to you whenever trouble strikes, and you will help me. Where among the heathen gods is there a god like you? Where are their miracles? All the nations . . . will come and bow before you (Ps. 86:6–9 LB).

April 19 began as a normal day for missionaries John and Beth Petersen. They spent the morning in language study, then Beth took two-year-old Jill to play in the pool.

As Jill splashed happily, Beth spent a few minutes chatting with nearby children. When she turned back to Jill, the child had disappeared.

With sudden panic, Beth scanned the water. No Jill. Leaving the pool, she began calling frantically. No answer.

Another missionary who was ready to drive away from the compound heard Beth's anxious shouts and stopped to help in the search. A missionary nurse who had just arrived at the pool for a swim dived into the water to look. Nothing. She tried again. This time Jill came into view, floating near the bottom of the pool.

Fear gripped the nurse's heart as she surfaced with the little girl and began artificial respiration. As she pumped the baby's chest, the other missionaries bowed in prayer. Desperate minutes crept by. Just when the nurse was at the point of giving up, she felt Jill gasp for breath.

The hospital was twenty minutes away and required that a doctor be waiting to admit the patient. The women had no time to locate a doctor, so they set off through the busy afternoon traffic. When they dashed into the hospital, God provided the second miracle: In spite of a serious shortage, oxygen was available in the emergency room, and Jill received immediate help.

In the meantime, one of the missionaries had set out across town to locate Jill's father, who was delivering some parcels by motorcycle. Together they rushed to the hospital, where they found that Jill had not arrived. As they turned to leave, they saw a pediatrician who agreed to handle Jill's case. So God provided the admitting physician before the tot arrived.

After two hours of intensive care on a respirator, Jill had improved to the point that doctors said she would survive. They wondered whether she would suffer brain damage. By the next day, however, Jill was fully alert. Four days later, she left the hospital with no sign of brain damage.

The episode profoundly affected the Petersens' Haitian neighbors. Instead of loud wailing and despair—the normal Haitian reaction to a crisis—the missionaries expressed their confidence in God and their loving support for one another. Seeing this, the Haitians warmed to the missionaries' message of Jesus Christ.

—Celia Picazo/Haiti

WEEK 6/TUESDAY

PAIN FOR THE LOST

As long as it is day, we must do the work of him who sent me. Night is coming, when no one can work (John 9:4).

A stormy wind swept the shore that morning in Dunedin, Florida. Its cold January blast disheveled the coats and blankets in which we were huddled, while seagulls overhead shrilly announced our intrusion upon the deserted beach.

"That must be seagulls floating on a log," said my father as he pointed to objects far out in the gulf. We raised our hoods to watch. But idle curiosity turned to apprehension when we saw bright patches of orange bobbing to the surface.

Presently, someone voiced the thought in all our minds: "Could that be a life jacket?"

Surely, no one would venture out in a boat today, especially since news broadcasts had warned the public of the danger of storms. But as the angry sea tossed the orange objects, we sprang into action. Our teenage daughter Dawn ran along the beach, hoping to find a car with a C.B. radio.

Our son Daryl said, "Someone's alive! They're calling for help!" He ran toward the water, calling over his shoulder, "Who knows when help will come. At least one is alive. I've got to go!"

Looking up into the black sky, I prayed aloud, "O God, we need you. Save Daryl and those people. Help them know what to do."

Other people began to gather on the beach. I begged two strong young men to swim out and help my son; but they were unresponsive. I pleaded with others to go for blankets and hot coffee; but they made excuses. "The car is too far away," said one. "I don't know where to look," said another. I couldn't believe what I was hearing.

Our daughter-in-law had waded into the surf. "Thank God, here they come!" she cried. "They can touch bottom. It's two fishermen, and they're alive!"

We wrapped blankets around the elderly men, blue from being in the cold water for over two hours. The impact of the moment swept over me: What a picture of the church today! People are dying without Christ, and no one wants to get involved. My heart had experienced but a fraction of the pain God must have known when He stood on the shore of heaven and heard His Son say, "I have to go!" Yet God sent His Son to us, knowing He would die.

The pounding waves brought to mind the challenging words of a song: "Rescue the perishing, care for the dying. / Snatch them in pity from sin and the grave."

—Faith Weber/United States

WEEK 6/WEDNESDAY

SATANIC POWER

Surely the wrath of man shall praise thee: the remainder of wrath shalt thou restrain (Ps. 76:10 KJV).

The first World Congress on Witchcraft cleverly captured the news headlines across Colombia. The event had been convened by Simon the Warlock, acclaimed as a man of distinction. Fluent in Spanish, English, French, and German, he had graduated with honors in industrial engineering and had served as president of the Colombia Development Council for thirteen years. His much-publicized plans included nightly rituals, with one evening designated as a "festival of magic." Astrologers and many other experts in the "black arts" rented sidewalk stalls to exhibit their sorcery and magic wares.

In TV interviews, Simon spoke of how witches and warlocks are now respected and treated with the utmost courtesy. But concerned Christians decided to lay hold of God in an eight-day chain of prayer, asking Him to dispel the forces of Satan.

Missionary Florence Cavender reported: "Great was the fall of the witches. The congress was a big flop—but with beneficial results for the gospel.

"Newspaper accounts had built up the people for a big event. But before it was over, the news write-ups took on a different tone. Such titles appeared as, 'Witchcraft, Bah!' 'The Congress a Gigantic Fraud,' 'Now Ends the Witches' Holiday.'

"One article which referred to the close of the congress as a 'languid ending' went on to say that the congress 'finished not with thunderclaps and other phenomena of nature as predicted by some, but with a heavy and prolonged downpour of rain. Several days before, the "privileged ones" had packed their suitcases and left for their respective countries in comfortable jets . . . their pockets filled with money obtained from simple people.' "

Not all was a fraud, however. Enough satanic power was manifested to prompt a radio announcer to comment that the congress convinced even skeptics of the reality of Satan. One article called upon Christians to "intensify the work of evangelization which dispels religious ignorance."

Perhaps the most graphic Christian response to the witches' congress was a large ad in Colombia's principal newspaper, with the bold headline: "Christ or the Witches?" Below were the words: "Foolish people are running here and there while Jesus Christ says, 'Ye will not come to me, that ye might have life' (John 5:40 KJV)."

Persistent, believing prayer caused God to "cut off the strength of evil men . . . and increase the power of good men in their place" (Ps. 75:10 LB).

—Alice Huff/United States

WEEK 6/THURSDAY

TIME FOR REPAIRS

Be strong and courageous. Do not be afraid or terrified . . . for the LORD your God goes with you; he will never leave you nor forsake you (Deut. 31:6).

Moving a family is quite a chore, no matter when or where it's done. But this was the third time in three-and-a-half months that we had stowed our earthly possessions into trunks, barrels, and bags for another long relocation trip. Larger items had already been shipped ahead. Now the remaining suitcases and the cage with the family dog were loaded into the little Daihatsu pickup, and we began to cross the mountains from Hualien to Taichung.

After driving easily through beautiful Taroko Gorge, we started to climb the first mountain pass when the truck showed signs of engine trouble. No amount of persuasion could convince the Daihatsu to go uphill; so downhill we went, all the way back to Hualien and the garage.

The next morning, with a repaired Daihatsu, we set off again in high spirits. We breathed a sigh of relief when we breezed past the place where we broke down the day before. The truck crossed the first mountain pass and was well up the second when the engine started to cough and sputter. With a final heave, it stopped completely.

We climbed down from our seats and stood silently beside the truck. Towering mountains were behind and ahead of us. There was no sign of a village, not even a single mountain shack. The convoy of buses that travels to Taichung once a day had already passed; so we were very much alone on a lonely mountain road.

We prayed, of course. While Lowell opened the hood to investigate the engine trouble, Rodney and Renae tried to comfort me. "Mother, everything will be okay," Rodney said. "Two young men who know how to fix our car will come along."

I smiled inwardly. It was such an impossible prospect. Yet, moved by Rod's faith, we continued to pray.

It seemed that we waited a very long time. The silence was broken only by the occasional clink of Lowell's wrench against the motor.

Suddenly, a lively group of mountain climbers rounded the bend. We exchanged friendly greetings as they filed past, though I mused that it was not the kind of group likely to produce auto mechanics.

To my amazement, two young men at the end of the line stepped up to the truck and offered to help. Pinpointing the problem, they had it repaired within half an hour. We climbed back into the Daihatsu, and without a whimper the motor purred right over the mountain pass, all the way to Taichung.

Rodney and Renae sang until they were hoarse: "Praise the Lord! Praise the Lord! . . . Great things He hath done!" Lowell and I would have joined them, but our voices were clogged with tears of gratitude.

—Naomi Williamson/Taiwan

WEEK 6/FRIDAY

WASTING YOUR BREATH

May the God of peace . . . Equip you with everything good for doing his will (Heb. 13:20–21).

When you pray, you may find it difficult to disentangle yourself from things that distract and hinder you. But it is always necessary. Otherwise your prayer will be thwarted from full effectiveness.

A lack of faith can prevent prayer from achieving its purpose. We may say that "with God all things are possible," in a spirit of mere religious sentiment. But to please God we need the faith that laughs at impossibilities. Recently, at a prayer service for healing, I felt it my duty to whisper in the ears of those who were praying, "Believe it. Believe it. Believe He can do it."

A lack of reverence also thwarts the divine reply. We must come to God in the dust, as Saul of Tarsus did, without a spirit of bravado. Our spirit must be that of the publican praying in the temple, smiting his breast, and saying, "O God, be merciful to me."

A lack of warmth can cancel the power of prayer. Cold, duty-bound prayers accomplish little. How saddened God must be when He hears us mention the salvation of souls and our own desperate needs with no more fervor than if we were referring to a crate of oranges!

A lack of conformity to God's will can obstruct the flow of God's answers to prayer. The children of Israel enjoyed a miracle route through the wilderness, as long as they obeyed God. Examine your life for irregularities in your obedience to the will of God.

God offers to deliver you from the shortcomings that would prevent your effectiveness in prayer. Do not be satisfied with prayers doomed for heaven's wastebasket.

—Walter Brentnall/Ireland

WEEK 6/SATURDAY

OVERSHADOWED BY PRAYER

He who dwells in the shelter of the Most High will rest in the shadow of the Almighty (Ps. 91:1).

We had just entered the attractive living room of a faithful supporter and prayer partner named Mary. Suddenly, she blurted out, "Bill, did you need special protection last October?"

She then explained: "Your prayer card is in my kitchen. Not only did the Holy Spirit compel me to pray for you while I was washing the dishes that month, but even in the middle of the night!"

Bill and I looked at each other. Then he began to tell Mary his story.

One day in October he had taken a training group to the town of Progreso, Ecuador. They parked the car on a hilltop and hiked down through the town for a day of house-to-house evangelism. A couple of the townspeople accepted Christ, and believers there were edified. Then they returned to the car and drove home.

A week later, a lay pastor from Progreso reported that some enemies of the gospel had wired dynamite to the engine of the car in an effort to destroy Bill and his witnessing team. But a neighbor had persuaded them to remove it before the group returned. As Bill shared this with Mary, we knew the turn of events was due to her faithfulness in prayer.

Shortly thereafter, a men's mission team from the States came to our apartment. That afternoon I went home to prepare their dinner. The strong odor of cooking gas greeted me at the door. We summoned the fire department and the gas company, who soon located the leak. We thanked God that the building had not exploded. Two weeks later, we received a letter from a relative who said, "I was praying for you during the week of the team's visit, that nothing would disrupt their schedule."

Bill and I also recall the traumatic experience of seeking God's will regarding a possible transfer to Spain. The deadline for our answer was approaching. Bill felt we should pray separately for two weeks, then disclose God's leadings to each other by October 1.

When that day came, I was still in turmoil. But while listening to a sermon that morning, I knew without a doubt that we must say yes to Spain. That afternoon, Bill revealed that he also knew we should take the assignment.

The next morning, our mission's prayer bulletin arrived. Opening it, I discovered that the request for October 1 had been concise: "Pray regarding personnel to be chosen for Spain." I believe that is why our struggle had ended that day—people around the world were praying for us.

—Lois Miller/Spain

WEEK 7/SUNDAY

THE TRINITY OF INTERCESSION

He is always living to make petition to God and intercede . . . and intervene (Heb. 7:25 AMP.).

Intercession is a spiritual ministry with a threefold involvement—Christ, the Holy Spirit, and you. Christ ever lives to intercede (Heb. 7:25). The Holy Spirit constantly intercedes (Rom. 8:26–27). But God has also ordained you to intercede in prayer for the people around you.

He has made a covenant with us, to work in people's lives when we ask Him (Matt. 7:7–11). But if we do not ask, the trinity of intercession is incomplete, and His work is hindered (James 4:2).

Christ prays constantly for us. He is at the throne of God, adding His divine "amen" whenever we pray according to God's will. He is himself the "amen" (Rev. 3:14); because of His sacrifice, we have full access to the promises of God. That is why we are told to come boldly to the throne of grace in prayer (Heb. 4:16). There the presence of the nail-scarred Christ will be an all-sufficient amen to our prayers.

The Holy Spirit joins Christ in intercession. He prays with longings too deep for human words (Rom. 8:26–27). He enters into our heart cries, deepens our prayers, and guides us into praying for that which He desires. Thus, He prays not only for and with us, but through us, as we pray with holy longing. This is why the Bible says we must pray "in the Spirit" (Eph. 6:18).

But is it not enough if the Son and the Spirit join in prayer? No. They wait for you to join them in interceding for the world. What divine mystery! What could your prayers possibly add to theirs? Yet this is God's command;

this is His covenant of grace. You are essential to God's work of winning the world.

Your most important Christian work is to join God's interceding trinity. Do not hinder God's plan. Go to your knees!

—Wesley L. Duewel/India

WEEK 7/MONDAY

NOT TO WORRY

Do not worry, saying, "What shall we eat?" or "What shall we drink?" or "What shall we wear?" For the pagans run after all these things, and your heavenly Father knows that you need them (Matt. 6:31–32).

With father dead, our family had tight finances. I approached college graduation without money for the diploma, much less for a new dress to wear. Distraught, I was reminded of Matthew 6:33, which says, "Seek first his kingdom and his righteousness, and all these things will be given to you as well." I realized that I was not putting God first in certain areas of my life, and I resolved to set things right.

Even then, no money came for a time. But on Easter morning, a fellow student came to my room with a check—enough money to cover all of my needs.

God began teaching me not to pray for personal needs, but to make sure that I placed Him first in every situation. If I did that, His Word promised that my needs would be supplied.

While my husband was imprisoned in China in World War II, I traveled across the United States on missionary deputation. God revealed in prayer a certain amount of money that I could trust Him to provide each week. Offerings at the meetings never dropped below that level; in fact, they were often well above it. Until one memorable week.

I had fallen behind schedule in paying my expenses for the week. But with three services planned for the weekend, I expected to receive enough offerings to cover the deficit. I received many signs that God would provide. For example, at one meeting a man confided that a frost had destroyed most of his fruit crop. He had to repay a sizeable loan to the bank; but after the next harvest, he would send us some money for mission work.

When the last meeting ended on Sunday night, however, the pastor took me to the bus and handed me a thin envelope. It contained offerings that were far below my expectations.

Moments later, the fruit grower bounded onto the bus. He thrust a check into my hand and said, "Thank God, I'm here on time!"

He explained that he had not been able to sleep the night before. So, instead of writing a check to the bank, he wrote one to the mission. Before I could protest, he exclaimed, "God never fails!" and hurried off the bus.

Indeed, God never did fail during that entire venture of obedience and trust.

—Florence Munroe/Hong Kong

WEEK 7/TUESDAY

THE MIND OF CHRIST

I urge you, brothers, in view of God's mercy, to offer your bodies as living sacrifices, holy and pleasing to God—which is your spiritual worship. Do not conform any longer to the pattern of this world, but be transformed by the renewing of your mind. Then you will be able to test and approve what God's will is—his good, pleasing and perfect will (Rom. 12:1–2).

A fascinating thought for those who follow the expanding medical use of organ transplants is the possibility of a brain transplant. Will medical science ever discover a way to preserve the brain of some genius by putting it inside another human body?

It is intriguing to imagine the changes that would immediately take place in the person receiving a new brain. That person would think and act in totally new ways.

Such a thing may never be more than science fiction. But the Bible speaks of such radical changes in the life of a Christian believer. Ezekiel quoted God as saying, "I will give you a new heart and put a new spirit in you; I will remove from you your heart of stone and give you a heart of flesh. And I will put my Spirit in you" (36:26–27). The New Testament calls this change a "new birth" or a "new creation."

Paul told the Christians in Rome that they had been resurrected with Christ so that they could "walk in newness of life" (Rom. 6:4 KJV). Sin's dominion was broken. They were to bear the fruit of righteousness.

Moreover, Paul said that Christians should have "the mind of Christ." We should think as He thought and live as He lived—not as the result of having new brains, but of having "new hearts." John Wesley understood this to be the very reason for Christ's coming and dying on the cross. And that aspiration is expressed in Charles Wesley's beautiful hymn:

> O for a heart to praise my God,
>   A heart from sin set free,
> A heart that always feels Thy blood
>   So freely shed for me!
>
> A heart in every thought renewed,
>   And full of love divine;
> Perfect and right, and pure, and good,
>   A copy, Lord, of Thine!
>   —William B. Coker/United States

WEEK 7/WEDNESDAY

HOW LONG DO I HAVE?

My task is to do the will of him who sent me (John 4:34, paraphrase).

None of us can predict our length of life. All kinds of unforeseen factors make our physical health uncertain. Disease may ravage the young person; tension may destroy the middle-aged; sudden illness may strike down the "senior citizen." The truth is that this may be my last year, month, week—or day.

Jesus said, "It is not for you to know the times or dates" (Acts 1:7). The important thing for us to know is not the *length* or *tempo* God has ordained for our lives, but its *drive* and *thrust.*

We may attain true greatness in the kingdom of God, even without becoming noted leaders or intellectual giants. Humble people may be great, just as Naaman's servant girl became better known than her master.

Perhaps I shall be called to hidden service. Perhaps my willingness to accept a post at the back or bottom of God's kingdom is vitally important to His plan. Or perhaps I may be one of God's "middlemen," who will pass unrecognized by the historians and biographers.

Regardless of my length of life or my degree of notoriety, it is vitally important that I accept the place God has chosen for me. Each link of His purpose must be strong in order to make the entire chain strong. As I am joined to others, I help to produce the results He has intended.

As co-laborers with Jesus, we are given tasks that regulate our life spans. As yielded instruments of His purpose, we cannot die until we have fulfilled His purpose.

Death could not touch Jesus until His task was finished; then death became a part of His task. May the same be so for us.

—William Gillam/Colombia

WEEK 7/THURSDAY

NO MYSTERY

All things are possible with God (Mark 10:27).

An alarming telegram sent the prayer office of our missionary headquarters into action: *Valerie Murphy has sudden brain inflammation. Murphy family return to the States imminent.*

Immediately, I sent the word about six-year-old Valerie to our prayer representatives. They telephoned their respective prayer groups, calling hundreds of Christians to pray.

Ten days later, Mike Murphy sent our office a letter with more details. Valerie had begun having intense headaches. Then she had double vision; she lost the use of her left arm; she spoke in slurred tones, as if intoxicated. Neurological tests showed that the right side of the brain was malfunctioning, and doctors suspected a tumor.

Mike hurriedly got the family's passports in order and booked plane reservations for returning to the United States. Valerie's doctors ran more X-rays and spinal taps; they could not prescribe any treatment until they could diagnose the problem. That's when Mike sent us the telegram.

Two mornings later, Valerie awakened without a headache. The double vision had disappeared. Her speech and the movement of her arm were normal. The doctors insisted on keeping her in the hospital for observation; but after a few days, they pronounced that she was completely well. The puzzled team of physicians dismissed her with the statement: "This is one of those mysteries of medicine."

Soon after, another prayer worker and I visited several of the groups that had prayed for Valerie. We shared the good news of her recovery. Time and again, we knelt together to praise God for answering our prayers.

Several years have passed with no recurrence of the illness. Valerie's music and personal witness have reached thousands of people in the churches, schools, coffee houses, and homes of Brazil. She became a member of a singing group whose concerts blessed audiences across Brazil and North America. Today, she and her husband Dr. William Hammerlee live in Pennsylvania.

I believe Valerie's remarkable story is no mystery of medicine. It is a dramatic, prayer-generated miracle of God.

—Alice Huff/United States

WEEK 7/FRIDAY

TARGET OF DEMONS

They cried to the LORD in their trouble, and he saved them from their distress. He brought them out of darkness and the deepest gloom and broke away their chains (Ps. 107:13–14).

Six panes of glass from our front door crashed to the floor. Startled awake at half past two in the morning, we saw Jacques dash in through the shattered door. He was no intruding thief. Cruelly oppressed by demons, Jacques was desperately seeking our help.

Jacques had grown up in a community infamous for its frequent occurrences of demon possession. Despite that evil environment, he had become a Christian and had enrolled in our vocational Bible institute.

In a dream one night, he saw a teacher of our school standing before him. On either side of the teacher stood a cat—one black, one white. To Jacques, they represented the powers of hell and heaven. A struggle ensued. When Jacques awoke, he found that his hand had been cut. He came to tell us his story, begging that God would protect him and deliver him from harm. After we prayed together, Jacques quietly returned to his home.

The next morning, we were awakened by a sinister demonic voice. Its fiendish intonations were unmistakable. There in our bedroom stood Jacques, his face contorted, with a machete in his hand and a friend behind him. Jacques said that his friend was Satan, and he would not allow him to enter the room. Two hours later, with a group of Christians surrounding him in prayer, poor Jacques once more found deliverance from the demons.

A week passed. Jacques reappeared at our door, his

face twisted with fear. We pulled him inside and persuaded him to sit down. Limply raising his hand, Jacques declared his belief in Jesus Christ. He then fell into a stupor, and we carried him back to his room.

All was quiet until the crashing of the glass the next morning. We prayed together, and Jacques was again freed from satanic grasp.

Jacques is God's man; but he is still a target for the evil one. Please support him and his fellow Haitian workers in prayer as they attempt to spread Christ's redemptive message here. They sense the desperate need to rescue their people from the power of devil worship and the darkness of superstition.

—Elaine Lain/Haiti

WEEK 7/SATURDAY

BRIDE-TO-BE

And we know that in all things God works for the good of those who love him, who have been called according to his purpose (Rom. 8:28).

With great anticipation, Joe and I returned to Simla after two years' absence. Out tumbled our questions about old friends, converts, and workers. Then we asked, "What about Tej?" And the answer sent a dagger to our hearts. Tej had married a Hindu girl.

One of our brightest young converts, Tej had led others to Christ with exceptional zeal. Though he was eager to enter seminary, his responsibility to his aged mother made this impossible. So he had settled in the village of Rohru, eighty miles away.

Our workers had visited Rohru three or four times a year, selling Scripture portions, holding meetings, and visiting house-to-house. Yet not one decision for Christ had been recorded there; to the contrary, the town seemed to be ruled by a spirit of opposition to the gospel.

In this atmosphere, however, Tej was able to win the favor of his employer and business associates. To advance his career, they arranged for him to marry a respectable Hindu girl. Tej did not learn of it until the wedding date had been set. He objected strenuously, but they bombarded him with arguments. For him to back out would be dishonorable, they said; it would ruin the girl's future. He was bound by his own Christian principles to marry her, they insisted.

Feeling the pressure of this dilemma, Tej met with the girl's parents to try to cancel the arrangements. They would not agree to this. Tej said he would go through with the wedding if it was not a Hindu ceremony, and if the girl would listen to Christ's plan for salvation and accept Christ. The parents consented, and the wedding took place.

Joe and I despaired for Tej. He seemed to be walking a dangerous path. But we did not reckon sufficiently on God's ability to work good, even from distressing situations.

After their marriage, Tej began teaching his bride the way of Jesus Christ. She opened her heart to the truth, embraced the Savior, and was baptized. To her family and neighbors, she displayed beautiful courage and sweetness through Christ. When her parents served the couple some food that she knew had been offered to idols, she graciously gave them her Christian testimony, then prepared a different meal for her husband and herself. With this kind of steadfast testimony, she has led her brother, a cousin, and three other young men to Christ.

Last summer Chaman Lal, an Indian pastor, visited the town of Rohru. Instead of being rejected, he was given a warm reception. A new convert helped him sell Gospel portions at the bazaar and arranged for him to hold an evangelistic meeting in his father's home. Though he is a strong Hindu, the father welcomed Chaman. When the meeting began, nearly the whole village turned out to hear the evangelist, so the meeting had to be moved outside.

A local couple brought forward their baby, who was scarcely able to breathe. After prayer, the child was noticeably improved. Word began to spread that Jesus had healed the infant. The new converts asked Chaman, "When can you come again?"

God is working in Rohru through the person we least expected to be His instrument—Tej's new wife.

—Ruby Black/India

WEEK 8/SUNDAY

PRAYING FOR WATER

The poor and needy search for water, but there is none. . . . I will turn the desert into pools of water, and the parched ground into springs (Isa. 41:17–18).

In Haiti, anyone who lives near a well is in an envied position. The forty-one children of our orphanage at Hostin understand that clearly. They have often had the arduous task of walking long distances with full watercans balanced on their heads.

The children often prayed for a new water supply. Then came the wonderful news that a missionary medical center would be built nearby. It would be impossible to carry water for that facility, so a well would have to be drilled.

But where could we drill successfully?

At the orphanage, the word *water* was written on the blackboard with other items for prayer. For eight weeks, the children skipped breakfast every Saturday morning to fast and pray that the drillers would find the right spot for the well.

One day Pastor Doucet, director of the orphanage, marched the children outside and stood confidently on a spot close to where the foundations of the medical center were to be laid. The children felt sure this was where the Lord would give water.

The well-diggers soon came and started drilling. Slowly, they edged the pipe down 50 feet. 100. 150. 200. Still no sign of water.

Nagging doubts came as our neighbors began to comment: "We drilled for 600 feet and found no water." "Why did you choose that spot to drill?" "Would you like our engineer's advice?"

Then the drilling machine broke down. It was nearly time to start holding daily clinic sessions at Hostin, but drilling had to wait until a new machine part could be delivered. The orphans kept praying and believing that God would provide water from that dry ground.

And He did. At 300 feet the water gushed forth—clean spring water, enough to supply both the medical center and the orphanage.

Since then, two of our neighbors have tried to drill without finding water. "What engineers gauged the position for you?" asked a businessman. "I would like to hire them."

Imagine his chagrin when my husband replied, "Our orphans prayed."

—Ella Bourke/Haiti

WEEK 8/MONDAY

WITH MUCH AT STAKE

Without faith it is impossible to please God, because anyone who comes to him must believe that he exists and that he rewards those who earnestly seek him (Heb. 11:6).

To have much at stake is a great aid to concentration. As a man sentenced to the gallows once remarked, "The prospect of immediate death wonderfully concentrates the mind."

Perhaps we have so little effective prayer in our day because those praying have too little at stake. When we think the outcome of prayer is of no great consequence, our prayers become polite, desultory, and dreary.

Strong, urgent desire is the wellspring of effective prayer. And we feel strongly about those things that matter desperately to us. We see this principle illustrated by many of the great prayers of the Bible.

Moses had thrown his lot in with a motley collection of former slaves. After leaving Egypt, his future was bound with theirs. So their welfare was a matter of personal concern to him. So he prayed, "But now, please forgive their sin—but if not, then blot me out of the book you have written" (Exod. 32:32).

See Elijah down on the ground, his face between his knees, praying through six dismal reports of "no rain." What makes a man keep on praying like that? Elijah had staked his life on God's promise. That makes for earnest prayer.

The early Christians committed themselves to witness to the resurrected Christ, at any cost. Jewish authorities were out to extinguish their movement, so these disciples looked death squarely in the face and they knew it. What a prayer they prayed (Acts 4:24–30)! The result: "After they prayed, the place . . . was shaken. And they were all filled with the Holy Spirit" (Acts 4:31).

If your prayer life is in the doldrums, I suggest that you do something rash for God. William Carey said, "Attempt great things for God. Expect great things from God."

What if you take the leap of faith—and fail? Think of the bruised ego, the humiliation of that. Yes, those things may come.

And they may be the things we need most. They are often the prerequisites to real usefulness in the cause of God.

—Ed Erny/Taiwan

WEEK 8/TUESDAY

THE REAL ICEBREAKER

As the Father has loved me, so have I loved you. Now remain in my love (John 15:9).

A lady in our Thursday Bible study once called God's love "the great melter of men." My heart agreed emphatically.

One might try to get rid of a block of ice by pounding it with a hammer. But the more one bangs at it, the more the ice is scattered. Instead of disappearing, the ice merely spreads.

Another method is easier and more effective. Instead of using a hammer, apply heat to the ice. The block quickly melts away, leaving cool water in its place.

We Christians continually seek to change the cold-hearted people around us. We're tempted to hammer away at them, using methods of human design. But Jesus said simply, "Love each other as I have loved you" (John 15:12). That was not advice, but a command for you and me, His disciples today.

God's love melts prejudice and hate. His love causes fear and anxiety to disappear. His love removes all doubt and indifference.

Intercessory prayer is a most effective way to demonstrate His love. Around the world, millions of people's hearts remain cold and hard. But God's love, evidenced through our faithful prayers, can turn these gospel enemies into God's friends. Let's use the real icebreaker.

—Lois Miller/Spain

111

WEEK 8/WEDNESDAY

GOD'S RECRUITING SERVICE

Ask the Lord of the harvest, therefore, to send out workers into his harvest field (Matt. 9:38).

"Lord, please call a missionary out of our little community," Mrs. Laura Thompson prayed. "Perhaps one of my own children."

Widowed at forty, Mrs. Thompson had high aspirations for her six youngsters. But none was greater than the dream that one might be called to missionary service. She felt deeply the need for more people to tell Christ's redemptive story on the mission field, so she kept making this request in prayer for many years.

When Mrs. Thompson died at age sixty, it appeared that she had missed the joy of seeing her prayer answered—that is, unless God had treated her to a secret preview.

Exciting news circulated in her community shortly afterward. Lois Henry, the daughter of a friend, announced that God had called her to missionary service in Honduras. So God had clearly answered Mrs. Thompson's prayer—but He was not finished.

At Asbury College, her daughter Mary received a proposal of marriage from her sweetheart. Coupled with it was a question: Would she be willing to go to the mission field if God called him? Dealing with this, Mary was confronted by a second question from the Holy Spirit: Would she be willing to go if it meant going alone?

She said yes to both questions. That led her to marry Bill Gillam and begin a ministry to masses of people in other nations. When Bill and Mary stepped onto Colombian soil in 1943, do you suppose that Mrs. Thompson sang with an extra portion of heavenly joy?

In 1956 they returned to the United States to assume leadership roles that often took them on world-wide travels. While on a two-year assignment in Haiti, Bill became seriously ill and had to return home. He died in June 1971. The following May, God surprised Mary with a new question: Would she be willing to go to another missionary field—alone—as she had promised earlier? She again answered yes and left for Spain, where she served ably for nine years.

God's answers still have not stopped. Each of the four Gillam children—Judy, Linda, Joan, and Rick—has answered God's call to service. True to God's Word, Mrs. Thompson's prayers have reached, not only to her children, but to her children's children. Prayer is the root of God's recruitment program.

—Alice Huff/United States

WEEK 8/THURSDAY

"I'M SLIPPING, LORD"

Unless the LORD had given me help, I would soon have dwelt in the silence of death. When I said, "My foot is slipping," your love, O LORD, supported me (Ps. 94:17–18).

While in college, I took up the sport of mountain climbing. It's an exciting hobby that mixes the joy of being outdoors with the thrill of adventure and danger.

As in most sports, the climber must follow several unwritten rules. The first is, "The leader must never fall." If he does fall, he is not a good leader. The lead climber should study the route until he knows every handhold and foothold, every crack and overhang. He must be a good judge of his own ability, of what he can and cannot do. He must know what equipment he will need, so he will be prepared for any situation. The safety of the entire climbing party rests on him.

The second rule is, "Other climbers must imitate what the leader does." They must use the exact handholds and footholds that he uses. Any deviation from the route can put the climber on loose, slippery, dangerous footing.

Mountain climbers are linked to the leader by a rope tied to their waists. This is their only assurance of security and, at times, their only means of communication. The rope transmits a sense of one another's movements through tugs and vibrations. Should a climber need help, he needs only to yell, "Tension!" The leader quickly makes the proper maneuver to save him.

Mountain climbing is much like the life of a Christian. All around us, we see people who are trying to follow an easier route; but Christ's way is the only way. We can sense their pain as they find the rope tied around them is attached only to thin air.

Though the way is rough, slippery, and often painful, we are glad to be following Jesus. We need only to cry, "Tension!" to feel the everlasting arms of Jesus helping, holding, and uplifting us. Prayer is our only link to Christ as we climb the mountain of life. We dare not allow it to become tangled on the rocks from disuse or inattention.

—Wayne Schock/Taiwan

WEEK 8/FRIDAY

IN THE MIDST OF TROUBLE

Though I walk in the midst of trouble, you preserve my life; you stretch out your hand against the anger of my foes, with your right hand you save me (Ps. 138:7).

For several years Gery Helsby contemplated leaving the Air Force to enter seminary. Both he and his wife Anne sensed that God was calling them to full-time service. As an initial step, Gery applied to a seminary in Oregon; his acceptance cheered them on. Soon the Air Force approved his discharge. So the family happily prepared to leave their base in the Philippines.

However, their four-year-old daughter Lisa began complaining of a stiff neck, sore throat, and headaches. She couldn't eat. She lacked her usual spunk. An ominous mass appeared on the left side of her neck.

Anne took Lisa to the hospital emergency room, where treatment was prescribed. But the mass on her neck soon doubled in size. With increased concern, the Helsbys took Lisa to a specialist, who ordered X-rays and blood tests. The tests confirmed that Lisa was seriously ill, and the doctor said that she should be taken to the United States.

But the following day the mass was even bigger. Anne and Gery faced the possibilities. *Malignancy, radiation, chemotherapy* were terrible words that filled their minds. That night Gery placed a call to his missionary parents, Meredith and Christine Helsby, in Taiwan. They immediately notified praying friends, who joined them in interceding for little Lisa.

Within days Gery was able to send them a cable that read: *Air evacuation canceled. Lisa recovering. All tests suddenly negative. Doctor mystified. Praise the Lord.*

The doctor who had examined Lisa every day at the clinic now looked at her with amazement. "Did you sprinkle holy water on her?" he asked.

"Yes," her parents replied, "the 'holy water' of God's children united in prayer."

—Maxine Dumbaugh/United States

WEEK 8/SATURDAY

JESUS LIVES

I know that my Redeemer lives, and that in the end he will stand upon the earth (Job 19:25).

"Those words—so beautiful!" mused Benedito. The young Brazilian was thinking about the message he'd heard the night he accepted Christ as his Savior.

A victim of alcohol, Benedito had responded to gospel invitations before; but each time he continued his enslavement. Reform seemed impossible. But the words he heard that night had penetrated his soul and given him new hope.

The "beautiful words" were *Jesus vive* (Jesus lives). This resurrection truth brought liberation and transformation to Benedito's life.

Has familiarity with this glorious truth numbed your sensitivity to it? If you lose touch with the Resurrection, your faith will be diluted, along with the wonder and joy of communing each day with the living Christ.

The Resurrection was central to the apostles' teaching. They could seldom refer to Christ without mentioning it, so essential was Resurrection power to their daily lives. And it moved their hearers to embrace Christ's new life.

Paul prayed that "you will begin to understand how incredibly great his power is to help those who believe him. It is that same mighty power that raised Christ from the dead and seated him in the place of honor at God's right hand in heaven, far, far above any other king or ruler or dictator or leader" (Eph. 1:19–21 LB).

Commune daily with the *living* Jesus. Walk with Him. Talk with Him about troubled people who, like Benedito, will find new life as God quickens their hearts with the "beautiful words," *Jesus lives.*

—Melva Clevenger/Brazil

WEEK 9/SUNDAY

FASTING

Declare a holy fast ... and cry out to the LORD *(Joel 1:14).*

"Then they will fast." Who said this? Jesus. About whom? You and me and all His church. And when are we to fast? From Pentecost until He comes again.

Fasting adds depth to prayer. Mere abstaining from food, without spending special time with God, is not biblical fasting. Fasting empowers us to prevail in prayer.

Scripture teaches us God's plan for fasting. It explains there are three times to fast:

1. *Fast when your soul hungers for a great need to be met.* If words fail to express all that you long to see God do, fast as you pray. When the need is great and you want God to bring new power to your praying, fast.

2. *Fast when you seek God in deep humility and repentance.* If you have a tremendous sense of unworthiness, add fasting to your prayer. When you identify yourself with the sin of the people you serve and plead for God to have mercy on them, pray with fasting. Esther fasted for her people and saw God's mighty deliverance. Nehemiah fasted for Jerusalem as he identified with his people's shame.

3. *Fast to discipline your prayer habits.* When you need to realign your spiritual priorities, you must engage in prayer and fasting. Church history tells us that Christians of the first century fasted two half-days each week as a regular habit. John Wesley exhorted early Methodists to do the same.

Sometimes God will so burden your heart that you lose the normal desire for food and sleep. At other times, He

121

calls you to fast by faith rather than by feeling. You still hunger for food, but even more for God. Because you are God's disciple, your prayer and fasting become a spiritual sacrifice to Him.

—Wesley L. Duewel/India

WEEK 9/MONDAY

VOICE LESSONS

May the words of my mouth and the meditation of my heart be pleasing in your sight, O LORD, my Rock and my Redeemer (Ps. 19:14).

The alarm jangled me from a sound sleep. Fumbling for the lever, I pushed it down. "Five more minutes," I groaned, snuggling under the electric blanket.

Suddenly, I awoke with a start. It couldn't be! The five minutes had stretched to thirty. Oh, no!

Frantically pulling on my robe, I ran from room to room, awakening the children. I desperately thought of ways to save time. *Our thirty-minute devotional can be just a prayer,* I thought. Instead of scrambled eggs and homemade biscuits, we would have cold cereal and toast.

Even with these time-savers, it seemed to take forever to hustle our brood out the door. "Finally!" I sighed, still flushed and breathless.

Only then did I realize that we had cut out devotions entirely. *Oh, well,* I mused, *we'll do better tomorrow.*

As I walked through the living room, the tape recorder caught my eye. It had been left on. *This ought to be fun,* I thought happily. Pulling the cord, I carried it into the kitchen. I poured myself another cup of coffee and settled down for a bit of entertainment.

But the tape was anything but entertaining. I heard a shrill, almost hysterical voice crying: "HURRY, HURRY, HURRY! It's almost time to go. Where are your books? WHAT! You have no idea where your library book is, and it's already four days overdue! Hey, why didn't you brush your teeth? MARK, why don't you TAKE CARE of things?" The tirade rose to a crescendo, ending with the slam of the door.

Tears filled my eyes as I pondered the atmosphere of the home from which my children had left for school. No prayer. No loving words. No encouragement. What a way to start the day!

Then a phrase from Matthew 12 sprang to mind: "For a man's heart determines his speech" (v. 34 LB). Bowing my head, I prayed with the psalmist, "Search me, O God, and know my heart; test me and know my anxious thoughts. See if there is any offensive way in me" (Ps. 139:23–24).

My half-hearted promise to "do better tomorrow" became a firm resolve. God had spoken to me through my own voice.

—JoAnn Dupree/Japan

WEEK 9/TUESDAY

GOOD-BYE

Yes, and I will continue to rejoice, for I know that through your prayers and the help given by the Spirit of Jesus Christ, what has happened to me will turn out for my deliverance (Phil. 1:18–19).

"Good-bye, little house," Bill said as we left for the hospital. Recent developments indicated that something was drastically wrong with Bill's health. But little did we realize that he would not see our home again. Tests showed that brain surgery was needed; and the surgery revealed widespread malignancy.

Many people prayed for God to heal Bill. But he is gone. Can we say that God did not hear? Definitely not. Today, Bill walks heaven's streets completely well and unimpaired. And in countless ways the final months of his illness brought significant answers to prayer.

Mike was a hospital orderly, a fine young man who knew nothing about Jesus Christ. Bill talked with him whenever possible. A couple of months after Bill was moved to another hospital, we received a letter from Mike, saying that he had asked Christ into his heart. After the funeral Mike wrote again: "I'm not afraid to die now."

Bill's last two weeks were spent in a convalescent center in Los Angeles. Even there God had a purpose. Maria was a young Spanish-speaking girl whose husband occupied the bed next to Bill's. For a year and nine months since an auto accident, he had lain motionless and unable to speak, fed through a tube to his stomach. Maria and I were drawn to each other. We conversed in Spanish, and she soon stepped into a personal relationship with Christ. During the closing days of Bill's life, I asked God to prepare me for what lay ahead. One morning I asked the nurse if she would like to hear Bill sing while she bathed him. So she listened to a cassette recording of him playing and singing.

An hour or two later, I pulled the curtain between the beds to be alone with Bill for the last moments. No need for a nurse now. God was there; angels were bending low. There was not even a final gasp. He just fell asleep in the arms of Jesus. His death was as beautiful as his life.

Now heaven is nearer and Christ dearer to me. Bill said good-bye to our little house, but he now occupies a mansion.

—Mary Gillam/Spain

WEEK 9/WEDNESDAY

CAN WE PASS BY?

When [Jesus] saw the crowds, he had compassion on them, because they were harassed and helpless (Matt. 9:36).

"How can anyone do this to an innocent baby?" I cried. Snuggling him to me, I ran from the small village of La Flor to the missionary compound in search of a nurse. Two months old, weighing three pounds, the baby had never been fed properly. His mother had died two days before, leaving him with advanced malnutrition.

Aided by a medical book and the counsel of our nurse, I set up an intensive care unit in my home. For three days I fought to save the baby's life, but the Lord chose to take him.

This experience opened my eyes to the tremendous needs around us. La Flor is a squatter community; few of the people own their homes. Landowners often exploit the villagers. And without a single outhouse in the community, the health conditions defy description.

Other missionaries joined me in visiting La Flor. Our goal was to share the plan of salvation in every home as well as instruct the new Christians there. In nine weeks, sixteen people accepted Christ. Since most of the new believers couldn't read, we began teaching them Bible verses. For children whose parents could not provide schooling, we began some basic instruction.

In nearly every household, we found someone ill. One young man who accepted the Lord died two weeks later, leaving twenty-seven children. Six were mothered by the woman he lived with, twenty-one by women in various villages.

The villagers of La Flor soon evidenced new hope about their situation. Sixty-five of them banded together to form a community development council, which strives to improve living conditions there.

But great problems plague the church in La Flor. With nearly all of the parents unmarried, difficult moral issues must be resolved before they can be allowed to join the church. Many are shackled to gambling and witchcraft. Hunger, disease, and other hardships hinder their spiritual growth.

Can we turn our heads the other way? Places like La Flor need to be transformed by the power of Jesus Christ.

—Celia Picazo/Haiti

WEEK 9/THURSDAY

GOD SAID, "GO!"

Praise the LORD, *O my soul, and forget not all his benefits. He forgives all my sins and heals all my diseases. . . . He satisfies my desires with good things, so that my youth is renewed like the eagle's (Ps. 103:2–3, 5).*

Raw, throbbing pain wrenched Betty Hollier as the car pulled up to the hospital. She had come every morning for treatment of her injured back, excruciatingly painful treatments that lasted five hours. But this morning, as she stood beside the car door, it suddenly seemed as if the Lord stood with her. "It is not what you feel that counts," He whispered, "it's your faith. Go and tell that you are healed."

The New Zealand winter wind cut into her as she shuffled across the parking lot. She felt troubled by such a clear command from God and her mind raced back to that day sixteen months before, when Ray had fallen from his tractor. The sharp steel blade of the plow ripped his back open, from his shoulder diagonally across the spine and down into his hip. He had been home from the hospital only a week when he broke his leg and was placed in a cast for months. Then came her turn. An accident put her in the hospital for ten weeks of traction, followed by five months wearing a cast, then a full-body support.

Ray and Betty sensed that God was speaking to them through these accidents. After much prayer, they decided to sell their farm. Near their new home they found a new place to worship. On their second visit to a service there, the pastor spoke confidently of the promise in Psalm 103:4–5. But how could the Lord renew her youth? Betty thought back to her childhood years, when she loved to do handstands and turn cartwheels; surely those times could not be "renewed." But she reckoned without God.

When the pastor announced a prayer and anointing service for one afternoon, the Holliers decided to attend. There the group prayed for Betty's healing.

Now in the parking lot, the memory of those prayers and the clear command of God converged in Betty's mind. She exclaimed, "Lord, You can't let me down." When she told the surgeon and his staff that she was healed, they looked at her askance and began the treatment anyway. But the usual pain was gone. After two hours of treatment, they let her go home.

That evening, Betty asked the Lord for confirmation of His leading. Praise filled her heart as her daily Bible reading brought her to Acts 4:10: "By the name of Jesus . . . this man stands before you completely healed."

That Friday, Ray was asked to help build a youth camp in Japan. Could she cope with going there? Again the Lord spoke from His Word, this time in Acts 7:3: "Leave your country." God proved His faithfulness, as they worked with missionaries in Japan for six months at their own expense.

Specialists had said that Betty would never walk normally, but the Lord has the last word. The Holliers returned to Japan as career missionaries, Ray to handle maintenance at the youth camp and Betty to teach at the Christian Academy of Japan.

—Robert D. Wood/United States

WEEK 9/FRIDAY

DIE CLIMBING

Forgetting what is behind and straining toward what is ahead, I press on toward the goal (Phil. 3:13–14).

Ever wonder what you'll be doing at age eighty-five? That great Old Testament character Caleb had no thought of settling down to enjoy his retirement. Instead of resting on his achievements, he asked the leader of his nation, "Give me this mountain."

What was the secret of his indomitable spirit? The Word reveals that he "followed the LORD wholeheartedly" (Num. 32:12). With no reservations, his active faith thrived in an atmosphere of total commitment to God. He was more conscious of God than of any problems. He knew only too well the giant-sized difficulties facing him and his contemporaries; but by being mindful of God's power, he viewed those giants as pygmies.

For forty years, he and Joshua had been surrounded by people whose faith was sufficient to take them out of Egypt, but not into Canaan. Yet he lived in quiet expectation that God would bring them into the Promised Land. When that promise was fulfilled, Caleb asked for the opportunity to settle the hill country around Hebron. The project seemed foolish. But with the glad assurance that God was with him, he successfully possessed his inheritance. Later he bestowed his benediction upon his daughter, who asked for springs of water to irrigate the lands he had given her. Where did the springs of water come from? They flowed from Caleb's mountain.

Do you have mountains to be climbed, giants to be slain, or cities to be taken? Has God promised you some inheritance that you have not yet possessed? It's time to review God's faithfulness and offer Him your consecration, without reservations.

As you take your eyes off your problems and look at His promises, you will possess your inheritance. Like Caleb, you will be able to die climbing.

—Stanley Banks/England

WEEK 9/SATURDAY

CONSISTENCY IN PRAYER

[We] should always pray and not give up (Luke 18:1).

When I was a boy I was not home much of the time. Mother and Dad were missionaries to India, so for nine months of each year my brother and I went to a Christian boarding school in the Himalayan Mountains. The three months at home always seemed to pass in a blur. Too soon it was time to pack our school trunks and leave again. But from those brief home periods a deep impression was made on my spiritual life. From six until seven each morning, Mother and Dad were on their knees—Mother in the living room beside the couch and Dad in his study—with open Bibles spread before them.

As a missionary, I have struggled to make my own prayer times consistent. One useful means has been a prayer notebook. Across my desk as I write this are several tattered notebooks dating back to October 1959, when we arrived as missionaries in Hong Kong. Through the years, these books have been good friends, helping me to organize my thoughts, record insights from the Word, and note my prayer requests and answers.

A notebook invites consistency in the devotional life. The clean page waiting to be written upon is like the day waiting to be lived. The ritual of writing down the date, going back to a prayer request and filling in the answer—all of these tend to form good prayer habits.

—Robert Erny/Indonesia

WEEK 10/SUNDAY

BY CHANCE?

The earnest (heartfelt, continued) prayer of a right-eous man makes tremendous power available— dynamic in its working (James 5:16 AMP.).

It was such a beautiful day that we decided to take the visiting youth group from England to our camp. On a whim, we took along the canoe.

Several boys used the canoe while others swam in a small inlet. A few said they'd like to swim to the other side.

A short time later, I noticed my wife's concern. "Ken's in trouble," she said. I looked and saw nothing wrong. But she kept watching and said it again. The third time I realized she was right. About twenty-five feet from the opposite shore, Ken was floundering where the water was at least seventy-five feet deep.

Grabbing the canoe, which had just been returned to shore, I paddled frantically toward Ken. A strong breeze resisted me, and I was still fifteen feet away when Ken went down. Diving out of the canoe, I swam underwater. I'll never forget that sight. Ken, whose arms were trailing lifelessly above his head, was sinking rapidly to the bottom.

About six feet below the surface, I was able to grab Ken under his arms. Only the Lord gave me strength to bring him up and swim to the canoe. Others came to help us; with six of us hanging to the sides of the canoe and with Ken draped over my arm, we managed to get to shore.

The steep, rocky incline made it impossible to beach the canoe. We had to roll Ken into the canoe and push toward more level ground. It seemed that an eternity passed before we carried him over the sharp rocks and laid him on a ramp.

Mark Wittig, a young missionary who had arrived in Spain only ten days before, gave Ken artificial respiration. Before long Ken was breathing normally again.

A sober group returned to camp. What if we hadn't taken the canoe that day? Why had the boys brought it to shore at the moment it was needed? Was it by chance that Diane noticed Ken was in trouble? And by chance that Mark was there, trained to give artificial respiration? Definitely not.

That week our mission prayer bulletin had mentioned the youth group from England. At the end of the note were the words, "Add prayer for the camp experiences." That added prayer brought results.

—John Turnidge/Spain

THE COOKIE CONNECTION

I can do everything through him who gives me strength (Phil. 4:13).

Several years ago, a prominent voodoo priest was on the verge of conversion to Christ. He lived near the church at Lory, where our family had worshiped for several years. So, of course, we were vitally concerned about the outcome. We knew that many people of the community would follow if this man accepted Christ.

Our burden for the man was very great. For days, almost every thought turned into intercessory prayer for his salvation.

One afternoon, I headed for the cookie jar. I love cookies. The only trouble is that I can't eat just one, or two, or . . .

As I reached into the jar, there came a strong conviction that I could not eat these cookies and still pray for the voodoo priest. *What*, I wondered, *could be the connection between cookies and a man's salvation?* But the conviction persisted for several days.

I finally reached some conclusions. The voodoo priest was a battlefield for the struggle between satanic forces and the Spirit of God. The same conflict goes on around the world, in individuals and nations. It is nothing short of spiritual warfare. Wars are made up of battles; and what happens in each skirmish affects the outcome of the war.

I began to see that my own fight against the sin of intemperance was connected with the voodoo priest's combat against Satan. I could not pray for the Holy Spirit's success in his life if I were not allowing God's triumph in my own.

God gave me the power to resist eating the cookies, enabling me to pray. However, the voodoo priest succumbed to the enemy's attacks and remains the Devil's prisoner today.

How could this be? We know that "the one who is in you is greater than the one who is in the world" (1 John 4:4). So why was the Holy Spirit not victorious in that man's life?

I believe that one battle was won when God helped me overcome temptation. But among God's children around the world, involved as they are in spiritual warfare, how are the conquests going? Can it be that other defeats weakened God's cause, allowing Satan to triumph in the life of the voodoo priest?

—Marilyn Shaferly/Haiti

WEEK 10/TUESDAY

ABOVE RULERS

Great is the LORD in Zion; he is exalted over all the nations. Let them praise your great and awesome name—he is holy (Ps. 99:2–3).

With a slight shudder, the VC-10 lifted off the runway at Manchester's Ringway Airport in England. We smiled meaningfully at one another. After four months of deputation meetings, five thousand miles of travel in Britain, and six frustrating weeks of international red tape, we were finally on our way to the post where God had so clearly appointed us.

As the plane soared through overhanging clouds into glorious sunshine, we indulged in a little retrospection. Six weeks before, we had been set to leave Britain for the United States. Our appointment: to work in the printing department at our missionary headquarters. On January 29 we had sold the last of our furniture and moved out of our home to spend a couple of days with friends.

The next day we received a cable that bluntly stated: *Visas delayed.* We were disappointed and perplexed. We felt no better when, a few days later, we received word that our visas had been denied.

What was God doing? Was this His way of testing our dedication to Him, or was Satan trying to deflect us from God's will? All we could do was pray, "Lord, let Your will be done. . . . "

Week followed week, and our perplexity deepened. Why had God let us come this far, if we could not go to America? Why had He allowed us to sell our home and put our loved ones through the trauma of saying good-bye?

After five puzzling weeks, we received a letter from a

friend who had previously been a source of spiritual counsel to us. He expressed the conviction that Satan was interfering with the plan of the Lord. He felt we should not pray generally for the Lord's will to be done, but should stand against Satan and claim his defeat in Jesus' name.

We began to take his advice. Immediately, Satan retaliated through personal accident and illness. But if he objected to our faith so strongly, we knew we must be praying along the right lines.

At the same time, we contacted our supporters throughout the British Isles, and they relayed word to prayer intercessors around the world. Hundreds of people focused their prayers on a seemingly impossible task—a reversal of the denied visas to America. Three days later, we received word that our visas had been granted.

As the plane climbed, so did the tide of praise in our hearts. As never before, we are convinced with Tennyson that "more things are wrought by prayer than this world dreams of."

—Stuart Banks/Indonesia

WEEK 10/WEDNESDAY

MOUNTAINS AND ALL

I was young and now I am old, yet I have never seen the righteous forsaken or their children begging bread (Ps. 37:25).

My heart sank as I finished reading the letter from mission headquarters. There was good news: I had been accepted as a missionary candidate for Haiti. But then came the blow: Before I could begin my career, I had to raise all of my financial support; and the amount seemed enormous. *I'll be an old-age pensioner before I get there,* I thought.

My parents had been missionaries to India, so I knew something about trusting God for my financial needs. Then my thoughts turned to my Bible school days in England, when God challenged me through the story of Caleb to take Him at His word. Like Caleb, I had covenanted with God to claim every mountain that stood in my path.

So now, letter in hand, I cried, "Lord, here is a mountain. Where am I to start climbing?"

To my amazement, pastors responded overwhelmingly to my request for speaking opportunities. Soon I had so many meetings scheduled that I wondered whether I could fill them all.

Then I wondered, *What am I going to say to all those people?* The Lord's promise came to mind: "Behold, I have put my words in your mouth." I studied to learn as much as I could about Haiti and missionary work there, then left the rest with Him.

I had just finished college and was receiving no salary from the mission agency, so I had not a cent to my name. "Lord, here's another mountain," I prayed. "But I believe

You are going to provide." He did. Every week during my deputation work, without fail, God sent me the money I needed—and sometimes enough to help others.

At a meeting one night, the Lord whispered, "Celia, a missionary in Colombia has a greater need than you. Send her the seven dollars in your purse." When I got to my room, my second thought was, *Maybe I'm just getting emotional.* But I could not sleep until the money—all that I had—was placed in an envelope addressed to that missionary.

The next morning, I reminded the Lord that He was rich and I was rather poor at the moment. I had just gotten up from my knees when I heard a knock at the door. The little boy from next door said, "Mommy wondered if you'd like to come and eat with us today." I had never eaten with these people before, but God used them to provide my food for the day.

That evening, while I was speaking, God challenged a young man to give me enough funds for the rest of the week. Another mountain was removed.

Several months later, I had to stay overnight at a youth hostel. The cost of the bed took my last penny. I had had nothing to eat that day, so I decided to read a book in the lounge to help me forget my hunger.

In a short while, I felt a tap on my shoulder. A complete stranger asked me, "Are you a Christian?"

I answered, "Yes, I am."

The young girl exclaimed, "I've been praying that God would send another Christian along! Would you come to my room for coffee and cookies while we talk?"

God spoke to both of us that evening. After prayer, I was about to leave when she said, "Wait a minute. The Lord told me to give you this money. I don't know your needs, but here it is." She handed me enough to take me on my journey the next day and to keep me going for the next week.

In less than a year after I was accepted for the assignment, I left the British Isles for Haiti. Walking with Jesus is exciting—mountains and all!

—Celia Picazo/Haiti

WEEK 10/THURSDAY

HOW LONG DOES IT TAKE TO FORGET?

Greater love has no one than this, that one lay down his life for his friends (John 15:13).

An earnest brother asked me this question at a missionary convention. I supposed that he was referring to the high inspiration of those days, or perhaps to memories of a visit he had made to the mission field. But he was thinking of something else.

"I mean," he said, "how long does it take to forget one's promises to God?"

He had made commitments to support certain missionaries, both financially and in prayer. Sadly, those promises are easily forgotten—and often are—after the missionary is gone.

If our missionary commitment is not properly motivated, it will not take long for us to forget it. An impulsive promise made on the spur of the moment, perhaps prompted by the engaging personality of the missionary, will not lead to an abiding commitment. The promise is soon forgotten amid other challenges and needs.

But what can keep us from forgetting our commitment to missions? We must remember that missionary work was born at Calvary. On the cross our Savior died for the *entire human race.* Jesus was compassionately concerned for the personal destiny of each individual, regardless of his station in life. He sought the souls of all men and women, whether they were attractive or unlovely, whether pleasing or irritable, whether receptive or resistant. We must give ourselves to the missionary task with the same impassioned abandon that drove Him to the cross.

In other words, we will remember our commitment to missions when we realize it is *something worth dying for.*

We are to be crucified with Christ. United with Him in His death, we enter into the very purpose of the Cross; our hearts begin to beat for the same world for which He died. At Calvary supreme love is displayed, and we are to be participants in that love as well as witnesses to it.

How long does it take to forget our promises? Until the love of Calvary cools.

We must realize what will happen if we forget the lost. Their blood will be upon our hands at the Judgment. We cannot afford to forget them. Calvary love remembers.

—William A. Gillam/Colombia

WEEK 10/FRIDAY

SIX STEPS TO SCRIPTURAL PRAYER

Pray in the Spirit on all occasions with all kinds of prayers and requests (Eph. 6:18).

If our prayers are to be complete, balanced, and biblical, we must be sure to give attention to the various aspects of prayer:

1. We should begin prayer, not with our needs and problems, but with *praise and adoration.* If we begin with our problems, we become problem-conscious. But if we begin with praise, we receive a new God-filled horizon; and from that vantage point all of our problems appear in the proper perspective.

2. As we adore God for who He is, we then *give thanks* for His gifts to us. It is not enough to give Him thanks in general. We should deliberately recall specific gifts and experiences and explicitly thank God for them. We should discipline ourselves to give thanks for unpleasant things too, believing that God's sovereign power can bring good out of adverse circumstances.

3. As we reflect on who God is and all He has given, we become aware of our need for *repentance and confession.* The Holy Spirit will convict us of personal sins; at other times, we are shown the social or corporate nature of our sins. What an overwhelming sense of responsibility we have when we realize that our sins and failures have contributed to the failure of the church and the general sinfulness of our world! Again, we must be specific in confessing and repenting of our sins. Then we can accept God's forgiveness and trust His promises of a clean heart.

4. With the certainty of God's forgiving love comes the quiet assurance that we can bring all of our *petitions and*

needs to Him. Jesus constantly reminded His disciples that His heavenly Father is much more generous than even the best human father. The conditions for asking are simple: "Ask in my name" (i.e., in harmony with His character and nature). "Ask in faith" (trusting implicitly in God's wisdom, power, and love). "Ask in love" (for a right relationship with God will issue in a loving relationship with our brothers and sisters). "Ask without wavering" (not allowing delayed answers to keep you from praying about your needs).

5. Beyond asking for oneself is asking for others, or *intercession.* It has been correctly said that "the greatest thing we can do for any person is to pray." Someone has described intercession as "love on its knees."

6. Every prayer should close with a fresh act of *dedication,* as Isaiah did when he said, "Here am I, Lord, send me." Prayer is more than turning all of our problems over to God. It is turning ourselves over to Him, so that we might become channels for His answers.

—Helmut Schultz/Japan

WEEK 10/SATURDAY

BEYOND UNDERSTANDING

God has said, "Never will I leave you; never will I forsake you" (Heb. 13:5).

"Dear Lord, where is my baby?" I pleaded. "Please bring her back!"

New missionaries, we had occupied an empty house in Bogota for two weeks until our barrels of possessions had arrived at the coast. My husband had gone for them. Alone with our two daughters, I sent our newly hired household helper to buy some groceries.

"May I take Christy?" she asked.

"It's about nap time," I said. "But I suppose fifteen minutes longer wouldn't hurt her. Just don't delay."

An hour passed, then two, and three. What should I do? The only people I knew in the strange city were my neighbors across the street. I went to tell them of my plight. Immediately concerned, they said, "Let's go look for them."

Together we searched the streets as rain began to pour and darkness fell. Four hours had passed. Bogota, always chilly at night, seemed even colder as I pictured little Christy in her thin cotton dress and light sweater. Surely her diaper was sopping wet. And she must be hungry. Never had I dreamed that our helper would walk off with my baby.

"O Lord, give me peace," I prayed. "My mind is in such turmoil. Why isn't Howard here tonight—of all nights? Oh, how I need Your wisdom!"

God granted peace as the words of Proverbs 3:5 calmed my racing heart: "Trust in the LORD with all your heart and lean not on your own understanding."

The police were notified, and Christy's apparent kidnapping was announced on the radio. Just as the traumatic fifth hour passed, Christy and Gladys returned— without the grocery items.

Where were they? I'll never know for sure. But one thing is certain: God brought them back with Christy unharmed—only very wet, tired, and hungry.

—Jan Biddulph/Colombia

WEEK 11/SUNDAY

DEVIL'S DEFEAT

The seventy-two returned with joy and said, "Lord, even the demons submit to us in your name." He replied, "... I have given you authority ... to overcome all the power of the enemy; nothing will harm you" (Luke 10:17–19).

Palmoo Das, from a remote mountain village but now working in Simla, became possessed by evil spirits after the death of her first baby. Desperation drove her and her husband Gyan to one Hindu priest after another in a futile effort to have the demons exorcised.

With hope and money gone, they related their experience to Rup Hans, a young Christian convert. He immediately responded that Jesus Christ could give Palmoo complete deliverance. "Come and meet our pastor," he persuaded.

The next day, Christians in the town were called to prayer. On coming into their midst, Palmoo was immediately stricken by her demonic tormentors. In an agony of distress, distortion, and exhaustion, she fell on the floor as if dead.

The Christians cried out to God, claiming deliverance in the name of Jesus Christ. Then the miracle happened. Palmoo sat up, her face aglow with awe. She had been set free.

Both husband and wife embraced Jesus Christ as their Lord. Many months have passed without another attack, and Gyan and Palmoo are among our most radiant witnesses in the Simla church.   —Joe Black/India

WEEK 11/MONDAY

INSTANT PRAYER

The Spirit helps us in our weakness. We do not know what we ought to pray, but the Spirit himself intercedes for us with groans that words cannot express (Rom. 8:26).

How often I have said, "I'll pray for you," as I waved good-bye to missionaries boarding a plane. Then, with the crush of daily responsibilities, I soon forgot my farewell promise. When I did remember, I felt terribly guilty; many days had passed, and I had not uttered a word of prayer on their behalf.

One day a veteran missionary told me how he overcame this problem. He said, "I make a covenant with God that whenever the Holy Spirit brings a person or situation to my mind—whether it be day or night, at work or play—at that very moment I will breathe a word of prayer."

Since that time, I have enjoyed the blessing of being able to offer instant prayer. Now I realize that the responsibility for remembering belongs to God. My part is to be faithful when the Holy Spirit speaks.

But let me warn you: Don't make such a covenant unless you intend to keep it, for God will remind you to pray at the strangest times and places.

Instant prayer also works in reverse. At times you may feel a desperate need of prayer support; perhaps you simply cannot seem to contact God in prayer. At that moment, ask the Holy Spirit to lay you on someone's heart. Then trust Him to do it.

I vividly recall an occasion when we felt evil forces pressing in upon us here in Australia. I asked God to alert someone to intercede for our situation. The feeling of oppression lifted. Later we received a letter from Irene McClane, a great prayer warrior for missions. She said that she had been awakened one night with a heavy burden for us and had prayed until dawn before she felt the load lifted from her heart. We learned that others at our missionary headquarters felt led to offer special prayer for us that night. I was not surprised to discover that it coincided with the time of our deep distress.

—Wilmer Brown/Australia

WEEK 11/TUESDAY

CONSIDER THE ANT

Our struggle is not against flesh and blood, but against the rulers, against the authorities, against the powers of this dark world and against the spiritual forces of evil in the heavenly realms (Eph. 6:12).

Cockroaches are not my favorite creatures. I shiver every time I see one. In fact, during my first term in Haiti I went hysterical when I opened my silverware drawer and saw them swarming everywhere. We had fought them for weeks. But that morning they caught me off guard, and I lost the sense of victory.

The ant is another aggravating little creature. Though not as ugly as cockroaches, ants give me shudders of disgust when I see them crawling our walls, over our beds, and between the sheets.

With these feelings, I would not have suspected that I would learn an important lesson from a cockroach and a swarm of ants—in our own living room!

I caught sight of the ants carrying a huge dead cockroach up one of the wooden beams. They were already two feet from the floor—some leading, others trailing, with a host of ants surrounding the body as they carried the load up. When they hit their first obstacle (a wide piece of trim around the beam), the ants stopped to determine their strategy. Carefully, they turned the roach so its antennae pointed upward. Alas, they lost their grip, and the roach dropped to the floor!

Were the ants discouraged? Not at all. Another small army on the floor moved into action. This time they carried the roach up the beam headfirst. They passed the first obstacle and began a long eight-foot climb toward the ceiling. There a one-inch bypass confronted them. The antennae crew began lifting the long insect's body over the barrier; but its weight was too much. It dropped ten feet to the floor.

The army advanced up the beam again, this time carrying the roach sideways. This worked for only a few feet before they dropped it again.

Back on the floor, the ants began removing parts of the roach's body to lighten the load. I left the scene as they started their fourth ascent; but they had already taught me a vivid lesson.

Scripture says, "Go to the ant . . . consider its ways and be wise!" (Prov. 6:6). Those little creatures persevered in carrying a mountain-sized load; they were strong because they united to lift it together.

We cannot face the battles of life alone. We are strong only as we confront our problems together on our knees.

—Valeene Hayes/Haiti

WEEK 11/WEDNESDAY

PEACE—LIKE A RIVER

He who dwells in the shelter of the Most High will rest in the shadow of the Almighty (Ps. 91:1).

In the fall of 1971, President Park Chung Hee declared a state of national emergency in South Korea. Intelligence reports said that North Korea was amassing military forces at the border. To counter this danger, Park called on South Koreans to devote themselves to the safety of the nation. "Be alert, be frugal, be watchful and loyal" came the directive.

Familiar with danger, the Christians of South Korea mobilized for prayer. Groups of fifty or more would gather in homes for intercession each day. Unmindful of denominational barriers or community differences, two to three thousand Christians would assemble for days of continuous prayer and fasting. Together they pleaded for God's protection from danger and death, asking Him to maintain their freedom to worship and witness.

Slicing across the peninsula near the demilitarized zone is a wide, fast-flowing river called Imjin. South Koreans feel that it forms a natural barrier, assuring their safety from attack. North Korea's heavy military equipment and masses of troops would be hindered by lack of bridges across this river, allowing South Korea's battalions to drive the invaders back.

But it was winter, and the Imjin always freezes. With its ice thick and hard, no bridges would be needed. So when the Christians prayed, they asked for a miracle: "Lord, protect us. Don't let the Imjin River freeze this year."

Reports from the demilitarized zone in early spring brought the news. It had been the mildest winter in the past fifteen years. Temperatures never stayed below freezing for more than a day or two. The Imjin flowed fast and deep.

As spring came, God's people in South Korea still gathered to pray without fear.

—Carroll Hunt/South Korea

WEEK 11/THURSDAY

THE SMALLEST PROVIDENCES

I will give you the treasures of darkness and hidden riches of secret places, that you may know that it is I, the Lord, the God of Israel, Who calls you by your name (Isa. 45:3 AMP.).

A dove with an olive leaf in her beak was all the assurance Noah needed (Gen. 8:11). He knew that a great new world, filled with glorious possibilities, was now his. Mrs. Charles E. Cowman, co-founder of OMS International, was quick to see God's smallest providences as tokens of His assurance that she could advance with faith. In 1943, during the third year of Dr. F. J. Huegel's gospel crusade in Mexico, she received a letter from him stating that another million copies of the Gospel of John were needed at once to supply churches that were catching the vision of evangelizing Mexico. Mrs. Cowman invited the staff of our mission headquarters, along with Professor Antonio Serrano and me, into her office to hear the reading of the letter.

What should she do? The mission's treasury was empty, and our plans called for sending the first contingent of missionaries into South America very soon. How could all of these needs be met?

Mrs. Cowman concluded our conference with quiet words of prayer. I don't recall specifics of that prayer, but she may have added the words that were often on her lips: "What Thou dost give us we will place in Thy nail-pierced hand."

With a feeling of assurance—yet wondering how such a colossal need could be met without any money on hand—we went back to our tasks. Mrs. Cowman did not go to lunch that day. She remained in her office, praying and waiting on God. When we returned at one o'clock, Mrs. Cowman radiantly told us her story:

"During the lunch hour a widow lady came in to see me. Before leaving she placed a dollar in my hand and said, 'This is for the Gospels for the crusade in Mexico.' Now that is a token from the Lord, isn't it? We know that He doesn't want the crusade to stop. We can go forward with assurance. He would not have sent His dear child in here with that dollar if He were not going to continue the work in Mexico, would He?"

She immediately ordered the printing of a million copies of the Gospel of John. As I recall, the cost would be $25,000.

She made no fanfare of any sort. She acted with the quiet dignity and soft-spokenness of a child dealing with a wealthy father, whose smallest indications of favor could be trusted. Such faith in action was absolutely intoxicating to the rest of us.

Oh, yes—the Gospels were paid for when delivered.
                                    —B. H. Pearson/Colombia

WEEK 11/FRIDAY

THE BUD, THE BLOSSOM, THE FRUIT

Let us not become weary in doing good, for at the proper time we will reap a harvest if we do not give up (Gal. 6:9).

A farmer may know what sort of harvest to expect by the color, shape, and size of the fruit he is sowing. But not the one who prays. The pray-er must put aside all preconceived notions of what the fruit will look like.

I had my first experience of rural life in northern Hunan, China, living with a missionary along the banks of the Yellow River. The simple Christians with whom she worked were like her children. I soon grew to love them. But I was quite dismayed by their dirty living habits. I had seen such conditions before; but I felt they had no excuse for being so dirty, since they lived so close to a plentiful source of water. I began to question the depth of their Christian commitment because I did not see the fruit of cleanliness, which I felt should be there.

Shortly before leaving that area, I spent two weeks in Bible study with the believers who lived within walking distance of the central village, where we pitched a tent. We were to feed forty people three times a day, as part of the series of meetings; and I knew there was no money in the Lipton's Tea box where we kept our funds. But the Christians themselves met our needs. They came to the meetings with a few sweet potatoes, small bags of beans, a little grain, dried vegetables, and flour. We had not asked for any of these things; they were the farmers' tithe of their produce.

Suddenly, my eyes were opened. I saw in their lives the beautiful fruit of giving. It must have been produced by the

Spirit of God, who gave His Son and with Him freely gives all things.

Let us leave with God the judging of people's hearts and pray with hope for all. Our part must be to trust Him for the harvest, which He shall give in due season. Let us allow His Spirit to open our eyes to see the bud, the blossom, and the fruit of His grace in those for whom we carry prayer responsibility.

—Annie Kartozian/Taiwan

WEEK 11/SATURDAY

SAFETY BELT OF PRAYER

"Because he loves me," says the LORD, *"I will rescue him; I will protect him, for he acknowledges my name. He will call upon me, and I will answer him; I will be with him in trouble, I will deliver him and honor him"* (Ps. 91:14–15).

Someone has said, "God moves only in answer to prayer." Perhaps that is the meaning of Ezekiel 22:30, which says, "I looked for a man among them who would build up the wall and stand before me in the gap on behalf of the land so I would not have to destroy it, but I found none."

That verse had special significance for me one day. In my early morning devotions, I was gripped with fear for fellow missionary Phil Chandler. He was helping to erect a radio tower, rising several hundred feet into the air. I reached out to God with insistent pleading, in desperate concern for Phil's safety.

A few days later, Phil returned to the compound, and we chanced to be walking toward the studio together. I remembered that morning prayer burden. "Say, how did your work go?" I asked. "Any problems?"

Phil flashed a quick smile. "None at all," he said. "Everything went as smooth as clockwork!"

I was nonplussed for a moment. Then I ventured, "I prayed for you, Phil, especially last Tuesday morning."

Phil stopped and looked at me strangely. Then he said, "Tuesday morning I climbed the tower as usual. I had to take along an electric cord, since I was using an impact wrench. At several levels I fastened the cord to the tower, so that its total weight wouldn't be on the wrench.

"At the two-hundred-foot level I stopped as usual to hook up my safety belt and tape the cord to the tower. My safety belt has two clips—one fastens to my waist, while the other swings loose until I am ready to use it. This time, instead of grabbing the loose end of my safety belt, I unhooked the clip at my waist. I passed it through the tower and snapped it to my belt.

"When I leaned back, out of the corner of my eye I saw something move. So I reached out and caught the loose end of my safety belt! As if it were a part of the routine, I fastened it in place and continued my work. Not until noon, when I came down from the tower, did I think of it again— and it's a good thing. When I fully realized that I had leaned back on an unfastened safety belt at two hundred feet in the air, I nearly fainted with shock."

Our paths parted, and I continued on toward the studio in a deeply sobered mood. What if God had not been able to find someone to "stand in the gap" for Phil that morning?

—Rachael Picazo/Haiti

WEEK 12/SUNDAY

LOVE IN THE PRAYER ROOM

The Lord make your love increase and overflow for each other and for everyone else, just as ours does for you (1 Thess. 3:12).

The golden text of the Bible says, "God so loved the world that he gave . . . " (John 3:16). Jesus illustrated the importance of loving God and fellowman by telling the story of the Good Samaritan, a despised man who was willing to give of himself for another. And Paul referred to God's love, "as Christ loved the church and gave himself up for her" (Eph. 5:25).

Even when missionaries find it hard to speak a new language, they can love the people. Paul told the Corinthians, "If I speak in the tongues of men and of angels, but have not love, I am only a resounding gong" (1 Cor. 13:1). Love communicates what words cannot.

Notice Paul's expression of love for the Ephesian church leaders: "For three years I never stopped warning each of you night and day with tears" (Acts 20:31). He told Timothy, "Night and day I constantly remember you in my prayers. . . . I long to see you" (2 Tim. 1:3–4). Love means giving yourself to another in prayer; and love in the prayer room has great power.

Last night I couldn't sleep. The lost people of Japan burdened my heart. Having just come home on furlough, I had left behind many whom I loved and longed to win to Christ. I felt helpless to show them the way to the Savior. But prayer became a bridge over the ocean to them. As I went to God in prayer, Japan seemed very close. Those were precious moments, and I believe God is already answering those prayers.

Prayer becomes effective when Calvary love breaks our hearts for the needs of others and lifts our faith to see their potential. May God help us to love the lost and carry them to the place of intercession!

—Stan Dyer/Japan

WEEK 12/MONDAY

A TREE BY THE CREEK

Whoever drinks the water I give him will never thirst. Indeed, the water ... will become in him a spring of water welling up to eternal life (John 4:14).

In Israel the wilderness area surrounding the Dead Sea is desolate and barren. Rocks and giant cliffs make up the horizon of that parched desert landscape. As I traveled there by bus, my tongue seemed to stick to the roof of my mouth with thirst.

At one place, however, the cliffs were broken by a deep gorge carved by a fresh stream, whose source is a year-round spring in the mountains far above. Lush green vegetation along the stream's banks is a sharp contrast to the surrounding barren rocks. Large trees along the bank send their roots deep into the streambed; the trees survive, even when the stream gets low, because their roots still reach the life-giving liquid.

The psalmist used the symbol of a tree to represent those who find strength and nourishment in God (Ps. 1:1–3). Like the trees along the stream, we cannot survive in this barren world unless we take our nourishment from God and His Word. With roots down deep in Him, we can stand so that all the world can see the greenness of our unwithered leaves. We can grow, sending out new shoots and bearing new fruit.

Our growth depends, not on our life above ground, but upon the depth of our roots. The tree itself cannot give life to the branches without nourishment from the subterranean water. As a tree has no life without water, we have no life without Christ. We must continue to drink from His life-giving flow.

—Wayne Schock/Taiwan

A WET ROBE FOR JESUS

I consider everything a loss compared to the surpassing greatness of knowing Christ Jesus my Lord (Phil. 3:8).

They hung on the clothesline, radiating the brilliance of Ecuador's sun. Once snow-white, they now gave evidence of the muddy river's toll. I counted eight of them. Eight baptismal robes.

But eleven people were baptized, I thought. *What did the others wear?*

The baptismal service had taken place in the nearby Leon River. Three communities were represented— Ucumari, Progreso, and Susudel.

The first five Christians from Susudel had stepped into the baptismal waters that day. It meant separation from all sinful social practices and, for some of them, separation from their families as well. A few months later, as students arrived to begin a new year at our Sinai Bible Institute, I noticed that three girls came from Susudel. I singled out one of them and asked, "Mariana, how did you become a Christian?"

"Pastor Nevio came to our house," she began, "and he talked about the Bible. We lived a terrible life. I knew my parents didn't love me. We had many debts, and there were always quarrels. My father drank continually, and he beat my mother and me. But he accepted Christ, and from that day his whole life changed."

"Did you accept the Lord then?"

"No, I didn't really understand. So Pastor Nevio continued to visit our home. One day students from Sinai Bible Institute visited Susudel, and I heard the gospel message again. So the next time Pastor Nevio came, my mother and I accepted the Lord."

"And you were baptized recently," I went on. "What happened then?"

Her big brown eyes lit up as she replied, "We all gave our testimonies at the river. I felt very sad for the way I had lived. But I was happy to see my father and mother, who were also being baptized. They had been so cruel to me until they had accepted the Lord. I had criticized them and always wanted to run away. Now everything's different."

"Then what?"

"Well, they told us to put on the white robes. But there weren't enough for all of us; so I waited until a few people had been baptized, and then put on a wet one."

"Did that bother you?" I asked, thinking how uncomfortable the wet robes would feel and how odd they would appear.

"No," she replied. "My heart was so full of joy that I never thought about it."

—Mabel Callender/Ecuador

WEEK 12/WEDNESDAY

A HIGHER LAW

Call to me and I will answer you and tell you great and unsearchable things you do not know (Jer. 33:3).

Dr. Taguchi, renowned blood specialist at Tokyo Children's Hospital, outlined for my wife and me the predictable course of aplastic anemia in our daughter Malita. His prognosis was grim. He said, "I suggest you not waste money on treatment."

Saddened by his evaluation, we trudged out of his office as if we had feet of lead. Dr. Taguchi's scientific report left no room for improvement.

Shortly afterwards, Mrs. Sekiguchi, a faithful Christian from the campus church, visited our home. Bowing deeply and with tears running down her cheeks, she gave us flowers and a card. Inside the card she had penned these words: "What is impossible with men is possible with God." She bowed again and left as quietly as she had come.

After being saved many years ago, Mrs. Sekiguchi had seen the mighty redemption of her husband from a prodigal way of life. So she knew that God's power is greater than natural laws.

Her visit expressed the essence of faithful prayer. Prayer is rooted in the fact that God is the Creator of all His worlds, so He is above His own laws. If He chooses, He can overrule one law with another in order to effect His miracles. What happens when a miracle occurs is not so much the suspending or breaking of His laws, but the operation of a higher law that we know nothing about.

When we pray, we believe that God is at the center— not somewhere on the edge—of the universe. Because God is sovereign over this world, prayer to Him can open possibilities as unlimited as His domain. As someone has said, "What may seem supernatural to us is very natural to an almighty God."

Mrs. Sekiguchi believed that what is impossible with men is possible with God (Mark 10:27). We experienced it. God's healing law superseded the presently known medical facts. Our daughter is well. Today our doctors have difficulty believing that Malita ever had aplastic anemia.

—Helmut Schultz/Japan

WEEK 12/THURSDAY

WITH LOVE

On him we have set our hope that he will continue to deliver us, as you help us by your prayers (2 Cor. 1:10–11).

The tunnel of our testing seemed so long. "Dear God," I prayed, "just let someone write to say that he's praying for us." I knew that many people were; they had promised to pray when we left for Colombia. If only one of them would write and tell us!

I thought of several people who might write to us, but no letter came from them. Then the following note arrived:

Dear Mary and Bob,

Please don't try to remember where you met me, for you've never heard of me. I am a middle-aged widow from a tiny town in Australia. You can't find it on the map, but God knows where it is.

I used to worry because I couldn't give money to missions the way I wanted to. Then God showed me I could reach the world by prayer. At times my praying seems futile, though I've been overjoyed that so often my prayers have joined those of many others and been wonderfully answered. I am still in the school of prayer. It is an exciting thought that God does not depend on my "good praying." Jesus is interceding, and the Holy Spirit makes our feeble prayers presentable to the Father.

I have often prayed for you over the years. Today there was a special burden when your prayer card came to the front of my box of missionary prayer cards. So I prayed throughout the day for your:

Marriage—that you will be one in the Lord.

173

Family—that you may be given wisdom and patience, and your children will grow in the knowledge of the Lord and be strong in body.

Home—that it will be a real haven to all whom the Spirit sends.

Health and Safety—that you will be kept from illness and danger.

Contacts with Fellow Missionaries and National Christians—to be free from tension and lubricated with the oil of love.

Insight and Wisdom—in contacts with those who do not know the Savior.

Protection—from the evil of this world.

Witness—that it will bear fruit.

Again tonight I am praying for you.

With love,
Lillian

It was enough to make me shout with joy. And God is faithfully answering that woman's prayers.

—Mary Sutherland/Colombia

WEEK 12/FRIDAY

WE CAN'T STOP NOW!

As co-operators with God himself we beg you, then, not to fail to use the grace of God.... For God's word is— ... Now is the "acceptable time," and this very day is the "day of salvation" (2 Cor. 6:1–2 PHILLIPS).

Christ said, "And this gospel of the kingdom will be preached in the whole world as a testimony to all nations, and then the end will come" (Matt. 24:14). It *will* be preached. God said so.

Who can fail to see events on this earth hastening to the great day when He shall come, bringing His reward with Him? But until He comes, we have a glorious gospel to proclaim. It is *ours* to be the messengers to every nation, to every tribe; it is a privilege committed not to angels, but to us.

God's order is always "forward." We cannot remain where we are. We dare not advance without God. God moves, but He never moves backward.

While daylight lingers and the night is fast drawing on, *we must work.* It must not be said that Jesus came and "found us sleeping." Because of the lateness of the hour and the enormous task committed to us, we must be alert and away to the ripe harvest field.

As we make our little practical plans, we forget that infinite resources are available to those who are ready to set out upon mighty ventures of faith. God's power is there, but He must have a channel through which it may flow. God seeks those whose faith corresponds to His resources.

Many things we cannot do. But there is nothing He cannot do through us. The challenge is to prove God and to do it *now.*   —Lettie Cowman/Japan

WEEK 12/SATURDAY

TIME TRIALS

No matter how many promises God has made, they are "Yes" in Christ (2 Cor. 1:20).

Big Ben, the thirteen-and-one-half-ton bell, strikes the hours in the clock tower of the Houses of Parliament in London. Each of the four faces of the clock measures twenty-two-and-one-half feet in diameter. The hour hands are nine feet in length, while the minute hands are fourteen feet long.

Squatting before that impressive timepiece, a lad checked his watch. The time differed, but certainly his brand-new watch must be right. So he said he would climb to the face of Big Ben and change those reliable clock hands to match the time on his inferior watch.

Can't we identify with his impulse? When our prayers remain unanswered, dare we ask that God's timing coincide with ours? Ophelia Browning's poem reminds us that perseverance and faith are part of God's plan in bringing answers to prayer:

Unanswered yet, the prayer your lips have pleaded
In agony of heart these many years?
Does faith begin to fail, is hope declining,
And think you all in vain those falling tears?
Say not the Father has not heard your prayer;
You shall have your desire, sometime, somewhere!

Unanswered yet? But you are not unheeded;
The promises of God forever stand;
To Him our days and years alike are equal.
Have faith in God! It is your Lord's command.
Hold on to Jacob's angel, and your prayer

177

Shall bring a blessing down, sometime,
   somewhere.

Unanswered yet? Nay, do not say unanswered;
Perhaps your part is not yet wholly done.
The work began when first your prayer was
   uttered,
And God will finish what He has begun.
Keep incense burning at the shrine of prayer
And glory shall descend, sometime, somewhere.

—Alice Huff/United States

WEEK 13/SUNDAY

TO GOD WITH JOY

Let each one [give] . . . not reluctantly or sorrowfully or under compulsion, for God loves (that is, He takes pleasure in, prizes above other things, and is unwilling to abandon or to do without) a cheerful (joyous, prompt-to-do-it) giver—whose heart is in his giving (2 Cor. 9:7 AMP.).

Last Christmas my children taught me an important lesson about giving. Each had saved a few dollars and with this meager hoard was determined to purchase gifts for Mom and Dad, Grandpa and Grandma, as well as each other.

The day finally arrived when Dad and the four children were off to the department store to experience the magic of Christmas shopping. An hour later, I saw the children reappear from the store, each triumphantly clutching an array of packages. Their faces were lighted with joy. At Christmas, when we unwrapped the gifts, their joy was complete; it was the joy of giving.

Mrs. Roberts taught me the same lesson many years ago. Old and feeble, she had been abandoned by her sons at a home for the aged. From time to time, we would visit her to read a psalm or two and have prayer. But one day we found her crying. She told how, after reading an appeal for missionary work, she had become burdened to give; but she had no money, not even a dollar, to give.

Upon returning home that evening, we slipped a five-dollar bill into an envelope and sent it anonymously to Mrs. Roberts. Not long after, we had the opportunity to visit her again. This time her face was radiant as she told how God had granted her desire; joyfully, she handed us that same five-dollar bill for missionary work. Hers was the true joy of giving.

Thinking of these two incidents, I am reminded that giving is meant to be joyful. This is not the time for painful calculation, worried frowns, or the set determination of duty. What if giving costs me something? That is part of the joy!

Neither is giving the occasion for self-congratulation. Let us rather recognize that giving is the most satisfying of all activities, and let us be grateful to God for the privilege of giving to Him who needs nothing.

—Robert Erny/Indonesia

WEEK 13/MONDAY

THE TRIPLE-DUTY DENT

Give, and it will be given to you. A good measure, pressed down, shaken together and running over, will be poured into your lap. For with the measure you use, it will be measured to you (Luke 6:38).

En route to a church service, my husband Paul spied a note under the windshield wiper of our car. It stated that a young man had dented the back fender while I shopped the night before; he gave his address and promised a payment from his insurance company. His honesty amazed us, for he could have left the scene without our knowing.

Our pastor suggested the name of a repairman, and Paul took the car over. He found the man under a crushing burden of guilt. A few months before, his nineteen-year-old son had been killed while working with him. On some days his grief gripped him so powerfully that he couldn't work. Paul became God's channel of reassurance.

While the man worked on our car, his neighbor walked over and began to ask him how much such a job would cost. This gave the repairman a longed-for opportunity to share his faith in God. He could hardly wait to tell Paul about the experience when he returned.

The honest young man's insurance check for $60.06 came speedily; but no amount of persuasion would convince the repairman to accept anything for repairing the car. Paul had helped a grieving father; the chance to witness had materialized; and we possessed an unexpected $60.06.

Unexpected? Yes and no. That summer we had pledged five dollars a month to support a fellow missionary; and we had done it on the principle of faith. It would not be paid from our regular allowance, but from other funds that we believed God would bring in. Without question, the check for $60.06 was our first full-year payment.

—Trudy Lund/Ecuador

WEEK 13/TUESDAY

THE BEST IN SIGHT

This is my prayer: that your love may abound more and more in knowledge and depth of insight (Phil. 1:9).

Peter's rich baritone voice rose vibrantly in my English class as we opened the class session with a song. He had chosen the chorus, "Turn Your Eyes upon Jesus."

Watching his happy face, one would never guess that Peter is blind. He was stricken at the age of seven in a remote village in China. While he played with friends, the brilliant sunshine suddenly turned to dense blackness. Terrified, he stumbled to his mother screaming, "I can't see! I can't see!"

Fear and shame gripped her heart. What had they done to displease the gods?

After a fruitless search for medical help, the distraught parents booked passage on a steamer to Hong Kong. They hoped they would find some way to be freed from this devastating curse.

On the humid ship, Peter searched for a cool spot to sleep. Curled up on a pile of rags behind some barrels, he was awakened by his parents' lamenting voices.

"Let's throw him into the river!" his father said.

"No, let's leave him on a doorstep when we get to Hong Kong," suggested his mother.

And so it was decided. The bewildered lad was deposited in a stranger's doorway. Later he was taken to an orphanage.

"How tragic!" we say. But Peter disagrees.

"Blindness is the best thing that ever happened to me," Peter says. "Without it, I would not have gone to an orphanage where I learned about Jesus. The things I see with my spiritual eyes are all I need to be really happy."

Watching Peter, I wonder how often my seeing eyes become too preoccupied with the things around me. How often I fail to see "the light of His glory and grace," as Peter does!

—Naomi Williamson/Taiwan

PARTNERSHIP IN MIRACLES

Make me understand what you want; for then I shall see your miracles (Ps. 119:27 LB).

Wendy pushed her way through the crowded train station at Taichung. On her way to seminary, she wondered how God would provide the money she needed for registration.

The night before, her mother had yelled, "You are foolish to follow God!" Her mother had often tried to persuade her to return to the family religion of ancestor worship. Divorced and angry, her mother lived in her brother-in-law's home.

"You come home only to get free food," the family said.

Wendy had retorted, "You don't need to feed me. God will take care of me."

After a previous argument, Wendy had moved her piano to her apartment; she planned to sell it and use the money for her seminary expenses. However, God reminded her that she must trust Him for her needs, so she returned the piano to her mother's home. Her mother gave the piano to an older sister; that sister and two nieces became Christians soon afterward.

Thinking of these experiences, Wendy was jarred by the sound of an old lady weeping. "What's the problem?" she asked the woman on the platform.

The tearful stranger said she had been forced from her room and had no money for a ticket to return to her family. Remembering that God's Word spoke of helping the poor, Wendy pulled the last money she had from her pocket. She used it to pay the lady's train fare.

"As soon as I get home, I must go to the temple and thank Buddha for showing this kindness," the elderly one said.

"Jesus Christ told me to do this," Wendy quickly answered. She then shared her testimony of what Jesus' love had done in her life.

Wendy soon stood on the seminary steps. She believed that God had "adopted" her into His own family now. Eventually, she received a scholarship. Weekend church work became available. These funds covered her enrollment expenses.

By reading God's Word and praying for courage to act upon it, Wendy has seen miracles happen. She has often been His partner in working those miracles.

—Valetta Steel/Taiwan

WEEK 13/THURSDAY

GOD'S DETOURS

Do not throw away your confidence; it will be richly rewarded. You need to persevere so that when you have done the will of God, you will receive what he has promised (Heb. 10:35–36).

Near the tip of South India lived a farm family who were deeply devoted to God. Though impoverished by the illnesses of both parents, they encouraged their teenage son Wilfred to find some way to reach out and share his Christian faith.

So J. Wilfred Dhamaraj enrolled in Allahabad Bible Seminary for six weeks. He was surprised and disappointed, however, when his stay was abruptly halted by acute heart disease. "Why did God bring me here if He knew I would get sick?" he asked.

But his teachers prayerfully directed him to rest his case with God. He withdrew from the school to undergo open-heart surgery and the months of required rest.

Rest? Back in his hometown, Wilfred knew anything but rest.

Eager to begin doing something for God, Wilfred gathered children from the non-Christian homes around him to start a school. The children quickly absorbed the gospel through games, art, songs, and stories. Proud Hindu parents began to display the artwork their children brought home. And by Christmas, a specially prepared program attracted seven hundred villagers.

With the offering given at that program, Wilfred purchased twenty-five chicks. Giving one to each child, he instructed them to "raise this for Jesus"—their own vocational project.

After five months, the children gathered their flocks for market. Wilfred invested the profits and eventually purchased a small piece of land as a church site.

There happy hands erected a bamboo frame and covered it with palm leaves. But, before long, the simple shelter could not house the five hundred new Christians of the village.

Today, next to the thatched hut, stands a larger building of white stucco. In addition to the "chicken church" of Trivandrium, Wilfred has helped to start two other churches in his home area within three years.

—Norma Jean Schultz/Japan

WEEK 13/FRIDAY

"AND IT CAME ... TO PASS"

Watch out for ... Satan .... Stand firm when he attacks.... and remember that other Christians all around the world are going through these sufferings too (1 Peter 5:8–9 LB).

"I am being baptized because I want to do the complete will of my Lord," Carlos stated earnestly. As he stepped into the waters of Ecuador's lazy Guayas River, however, he could not have guessed the trial that loomed before him.

Carlos deeply loved his only son, Carlos, Jr. And the twelve-year-old obeyed him well. But one afternoon Carlos sent the boy to a corner store, and he did not return. Carlos finally went looking for his loitering son. Irritation turned to concern when he could not find the boy anywhere in the neighborhood.

Police joined in the search. But the next evening Carlos stood before his friends at church, tears glistening in his eyes. "It's an attack of Satan," he declared.

Believers prayed for the little boy. We alerted our prayer partners in the United States and Australia.

Two weeks later, the futile hunt continued. "Carlos has lost his son," neighbors said. Their wagging tongues attacked his faith; but he clung to God's promise: "Fret not thyself because of evildoers. . . . Commit thy way unto the LORD; trust also in him; and he shall bring it to pass" (Ps. 37:1, 5 KJV).

When four weeks had passed, Carlos prayed desperately for an answer. He awakened abruptly at three-thirty the next morning, remembering a photo that they had of Carlos, Jr. In a tiny niche, he found the small cracked photo and rushed it to the local newspaper office.

Seven weeks after little Carlos disappeared, the creaky door of their home flew open, and a thin, ragged, barefoot boy stumbled in. Between sobs Carlos, Jr., told his story.

A well-dressed man in a shiny car had offered him a ride to the store. But at the edge of the city Carlos was blindfolded and taken to a remote hacienda. Robbed of his shoes, given very little food and no change of clothing, he was forced to care for the pigs. He knew no way to escape.

Several weeks later, his abductor's attitude suddenly changed. Blindfolding the boy again, he drove him back to the edge of Guayaquil. Then, snatching the band from Carlos' eyes, he opened the car door and pointed to a newspaper on the seat. Carlos, Jr., gasped at the sight of his own picture.

The young father embraced his son, deeply aware that God had answered their prayers and thwarted the evil that Satan had intended for them.

—Lois Miller/Ecuador

WEEK 13/SATURDAY

NOT ISOLATED FROM GOD

It is God who works in you to will and to act according to his good purpose (Phil. 2:13).

The coral-studded coast of Erabu Island was breathtaking. Miss Shinzato watched the setting sun cast red and purple spears across the sky. Since earliest childhood, she had been fascinated by the wonders of nature.

For years, she searched for life's answers in the study of natural science—always to be disappointed. Someone gave her a Bible, saying that it would end her quest for the meaning of life; but she found the language beyond her comprehension.

Then came the day she was attracted to a church in Naha, Okinawa. Like the morning sun, the words of John 14:6 brightened her horizon: "I am the way and the truth and the life." Suddenly, she realized that the secrets of the cosmos would be resolved by knowing personally its Creator. Right then, at nineteen years of age, she yielded her heart to Christ.

Soon after her conversion, she felt God's call to a preaching ministry. After struggling with this call for six months, she entered Tokyo Biblical Seminary. How grateful she was for three years of study there, which built the lessons of God's Word into her life. And upon graduation she was assigned to beautiful Erabu Island.

The first years were painful. She ran a nursery all day in order to attract the interest of mothers. She visited, witnessed, counseled, and preached in the evenings until she was physically exhausted. When she went to her first annual ministerial conference, she was determined to resign.

At the conference, however, she learned that her needs would be presented to other Christians through a worldwide prayer network. She would be linked through prayer with thousands of believers around the globe. She was not alone in her ministry after all.

As prayer warriors began to lift Erabu Island to the Lord, amazing things began to happen. Financial gifts from abroad made possible the purchase of a car for traveling to her ten preaching points. Several schoolteachers were converted, and they led others to Christ. Her high-school class grew to over thirty students; many of them accepted Christ and began witnessing to others.

Since Miss Shinzato could not reach the forty thousand islanders by herself, God gave her the vision to start a training program for twenty Sunday school teachers and Bible class workers, who went out to evangelize the forty-two villages of the island. Soon she established a summer camp for strengthening the new Christians won through their efforts.

As the sun dipped below the horizon, Miss Shinzato picked her way homeward along the darkened path. God was working on the island in fantastic ways—all because prayer had been multiplied on her behalf.

—Stan Dyer/Japan